101 VIOLIN TIPS

STUFF ALL THE PROS KNOW AND USE

BY ANGELA SCHMIDT

ISBN 978-1-4584-2518-8

HAL•LEONARD® CORPORATION

7777 W. BLUEMOUND RD. P.O. BOX 13819 MILWAUKEE, WI 53213

In Australia Contact:
Hal Leonard Australia Pty. Ltd.
4 Lentara Court
Cheltenham, Victoria, 3192 Australia
Email: ausadmin@halleonard.com.au

Visit Hal Leonard Online at
www.halleonard.com

TABLE OF CONTENTS

1 THE VIOLIN AND BOW (HANDLE WITH CARE)

The violin is a fragile, hollow instrument usually made of maple and pine. It is normally 14 inches from the button to the scroll. The top (front) and back panels are slightly curved. The tailpiece and pegs are customarily made of ebony or rosewood. Be very careful when handling the violin and all its delicate parts, especially around the bridge area. The bridge is moveable (not glued in place), and can warp or break. Turning the pegs without prior knowledge can result in breaking a string. If you need to carry the violin, grasp it firmly around the neck, and cradle it under your other arm. (Holding under its shoulder with your other hand is called "rest position.")

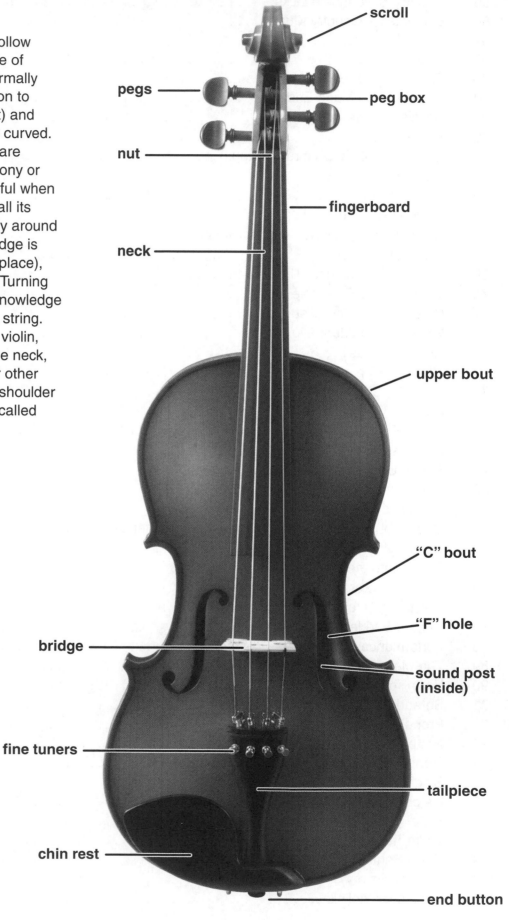

scroll

pegs

peg box

nut

fingerboard

neck

upper bout

"C" bout

"F" hole

bridge

sound post (inside)

fine tuners

tailpiece

chin rest

end button

Rest position, standing

Playing position, standing

Rest position, sitting

Playing position, sitting

2 STRINGS (YOU GET WHAT YOU PAY FOR)

Strings can have a variety of materials in the core and winding, including steel, gut (sheep or cat intestine), synthetic, etc. Gut strings usually have the richest tone but are more susceptible to tuning issues. A set of full-size violin strings can cost from about $10 to more than $50. Super Sensitive "Red Label" is a popular brand for beginners because of durability and affordability. Peter Infeld (by Thomastik), Dominant, Pirastro, and Helicore (by D'Addario) are generally considered a step up, and worth the price for a better tone. Compare prices online and at your local music dealer. Remember that a music store can install the strings for you.

Strings come in a variety of tensions: low, medium, and high. Low or medium tension is generally recommended for an instrument that has a very bright sound. Conversely, if your violin has a very mellow tone, you can brighten up the sound with higher tension strings. Keep in mind that, like a bicycle saddle, after long use your comfort will be a higher priority.

The E string is the highest and often the brightest sounding. It tends to break the most often, and can have an unfortunate shrill, whistling sound. E strings are often plated in silver, gold, platinum, etc. Companies such D'Addario (Kaplan Solutions E) sell "non-whistling" E strings to help solve the problem. Another strategy to avoid whistles and scratchy sounds is to use a very straight bow stroke and lighten up the pressure on the A and E. For more on violin tone, see Tip 90.

INSTALLING STRINGS

When replacing a string, you must first remove the old one. (You knew that.) Next, if there is a fine tuner – most violins have them at least on the E string – loosen the fine tuner several turns and apply graphite (pencil) to the groove at the nut, bridge, and fine tuner. Like engine lube, the graphite helps prevent future breakage. Bend the top of the string at a right angle about a centimeter from the top. Set the violin on your lap facing you and thread the top of the string into the corresponding peg. This can be difficult, because the peg box gets smaller at the top. When winding, turn the peg slowly while feeding in the string. Do not drop the violin! Make sure the string doesn't cross over itself in the peg box. Wind it toward the outside of the peg box. Hold the string in place and hook the ball end at the tailpiece – in the fine tuner if you have one; otherwise, in the tailpiece hole. Many E strings have a ring instead of a ball end. In this case, put the ring around the top of the fine tuner. Before the string has a pitch, when it's still loose and floppy, line it up with the appropriate bridge notch and tighten very slowly. Do not tune the string higher than the proper pitch, but gradually approach it from below. If the same string keeps breaking, and possibly at the same spot, take it to a repair shop and they may find a burr.

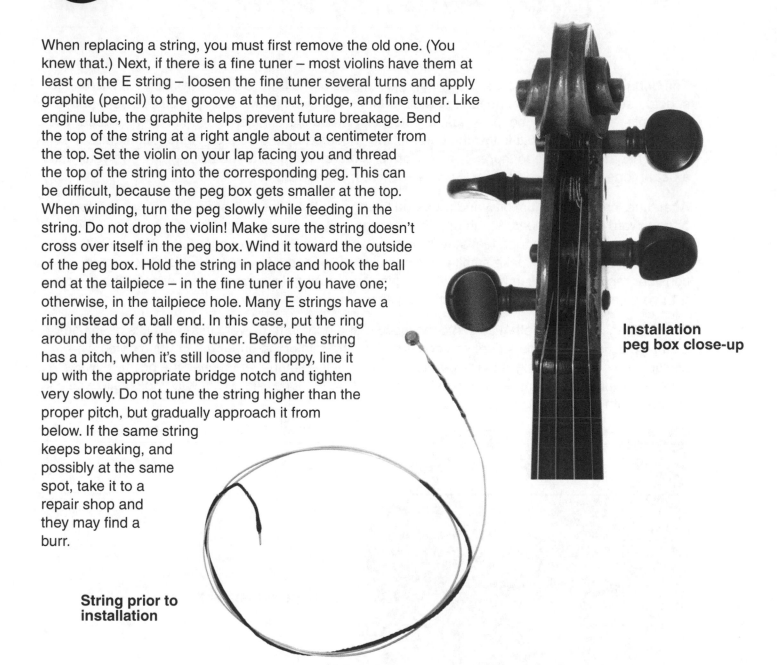

Installation peg box close-up

String prior to installation

7

4 LONDON BRIDGE (NOT FALLING DOWN)

The bridge feet should be located between the notches of the f-holes on the front panel. The bridge should rise straight up from the feet, or a bit further back, away from the fingerboard. If your bridge was replaced, there may be markings on your violin where the original bridge feet were placed. The shape of the bridge should follow the curve of the fingerboard, and be a bit higher at the thicker strings because they need more room to vibrate. A more ornately carved bridge may give your violin a better tone quality, but will most likely need more maintenance.

After time, changes in humidity, and repeated tuning with the pegs, the bridge often warps, most often toward the fingerboard. If the problem isn't too severe, you can try adjusting it yourself. Be careful: Make sure the bridge feet stay in place. Gently push with your fingertips at the top of the bridge. You may need to make small adjustments to the bridge a few times. If it is very warped, consider replacing. You can help prevent warping by pressing down gently on the top of the bridge with your fingertips when you tighten the peg as you tune.

The E string is so thin it often cuts into the wood of the bridge. To prevent this, violinists often use a small plastic tube on the string, and some bridges are reinforced under the E string notch. The plastic tube on the E string is placed around the part of the string that touches the bridge. Always situate the tube so that the excess plastic hangs toward the tuner side. That way, the plastic won't interfere with your playing.

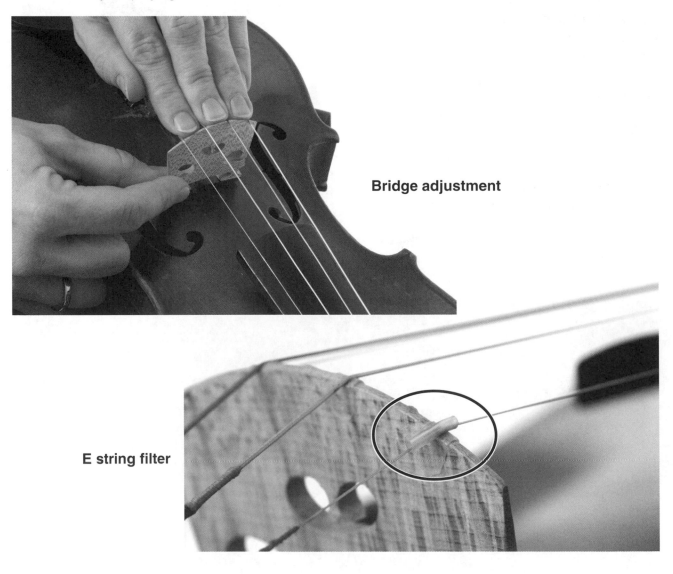

Bridge adjustment

E string filter

5 PLAYING ACTION

Playing on a violin with a bridge that is too high can be painful. Check the playing action (string height) at the nut and the bridge. Have an experienced player check to see if the action is too high. Keep in mind that playing in a fiddle style often includes a lower bridge, allowing for double stops (chords). If the action is too low, a string may buzz against the fingerboard when you play in high positions. Sometimes the action may be faulty only on the G string or E string. The E string is so thin it tends to cut into the bridge the most. This is why the E string usually comes with a filter at its contact spot on the bridge. Play in the full range of the violin to make sure the action doesn't compromise certain pitches. The string notches should be evenly spaced (like on the front cover) across the bridge top, with the strings resting on top of the bridge. If the notches are at the correct depth, you can feel the strings on top of the bridge, like bumps. If the strings are sunken into the notches, the bridge could be sanded/shaved down a bit so the notches aren't so deep. Try this before you replace your bridge.

6 TAKE A BOW!

Professional players typically use a wood bow with a high-quality Pernambuco stick. The lesser wood bows are often made with Brazilwood. The cheapest beginner-level bow usually has a fiberglass stick. Carbon fiber bows are very durable and are often used in alternative (non-classical) styles. They are available in different levels, from student to professional. Carbon fiber bows have grown in popularity as the Pernambuco wood has become scarce.

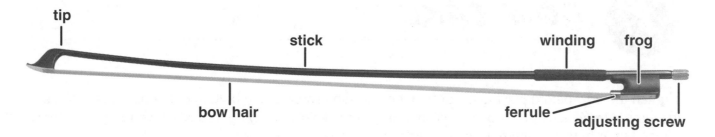

tip

stick

winding   frog

bow hair

ferrule

adjusting screw

7 NO HORSING AROUND

Horsehair is far superior in tone to synthetic. Since horsehair is more expensive, a good student-level option is real horsehair but with a fiberglass stick. The higher quality bows feature mother-of-pearl trim, a leather grip, and metal winding. The less expensive bows have a plastic grip and no winding. The figure below shows a close-up comparison of inexpensive vs. higher quality bow.

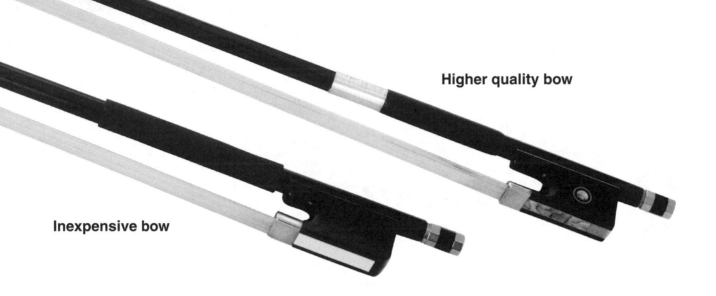

Higher quality bow

Inexpensive bow

8 BOW CARE

Tighten the bow before playing by turning the adjusting screw at the bottom of the bow three to five full turns. Always loosen the bow tension after you are finished playing. You will have to tighten more during hotter and more humid weather, and less when it is cooler/drier.

When tight, the hair should be away from the stick at about the width of your pinky. If the bow stick is not slightly curved in the middle toward the hair, your bow is too tight and/or the stick is warped. Avoid touching the bow hair, because natural skin oils will ruin the rosin retention. Wipe the stick clean of rosin periodically. Don't bother wiping off the hair only to add rosin later. If a hair comes loose, carefully cut it off with scissors. Ripping the hair out of the bow can cause more hairs to come loose.

9 ROSIN UP THE BOW

Rosin is a resin used on the bow hair to create friction on the strings. Packaged in cakes, rosin is necessary for the string to make a sound. Rub rosin in the bow hair about every other time you play. A new bow (or recently re-haired bow) may need more rosin. Rosin application lightens the bow hair. To avoid excess rosin dust, swipe the last few strokes in the same direction on the hair. Keep your rosin on the floor or in your case, not on your music stand. If rosin falls onto the floor, it can crumble into many useless pieces.

Rosin can be many shades of yellow, amber, red, green, etc. Violin rosin is usually lighter and has a harder consistency than cello or bass rosin. Some better-quality rosin brands include Hill, Pirastro, Andrea, Millant-Deroux, and Jade. Super Sensitive (Clarity) and Pierre Guillaume are among the brands of hypo-allergenic rosin for players who have allergies.

Cooking Tip: Rosin that has cracked into pieces can be wrapped in aluminum foil and baked back into shape in the oven. Although this may salvage the rosin and save you money, it can stink up the whole house. Warning: Many rosin cakes come in a very flammable wrap.

10 TUNING MATTERS (THREE WAYS)

Properly tuning any stringed instrument is one of the most important aspects of playing. The violin is tuned to E, A, D, and G from top to bottom.

Teaching Tip: From bottom to top, the violin string names can be memorized with "Good Days Are Enjoyable."

Many players use a tuner, pitch pipe, or keyboard as a reference. Use a tuner, tuning fork, or keyboard for the A string only, then try to tune the rest by ear like the professionals. You can check after you're done with a keyboard or tuner. The violin A string is the first A above middle C on the piano. Since the violin is tuned in fifths, it should sound like "Twinkle, Twinkle, Little Star" if you play G-G-D-D. It should again sound like "Twinkle, Twinkle, Little Star" if you play D-D-A-A, etc. Try humming or singing the pitches for ear training.

TRACK 1

The music example above shows the open-string notes on the staff. Tune these carefully, starting with the A as notated. Use the A at the beginning of the CD Track as a reference to tune your A string. Then stop the CD player, tune each string by ear, then check your pitches against the CD.

Turning the pegs
Turning the pegs for the first time can be dangerous. First turn the corresponding fine tuner down, counter-clockwise, several turns. Then turn the peg down, toward you, until you hear a click. Next, slowly turn the peg up to the proper pitch while plucking the string with your thumb. Do not let go of the peg until you have made it stick into the peg box. Never turn the peg up without first loosening.

Stuck Peg Tip: If you really can't turn that stuck peg at all, wrap a cloth around the pegs and carefully use pliers over the cloth to turn the peg down and away from the peg box. If your stuck peg is a nuisance, try a peg compound such as the Hill brand.

Slipping Peg Tip: "Peg dope" is a waxy substance that can be applied to the tuning peg where it meets the peg box. It increases friction and prevents slipping. It comes in three varieties: in a small container similar to a lipstick, in a bottle, or in a block form.

If you are purchasing new pegs, check out Knilling Perfection Planetary Pegs and the Finetune Peg (made by Wittner). They are called "geared" pegs and are generally made of composite material; they are easier to use when tuning.

11 DOUBLE STOPS

Most violinists and violists tune their strings by playing double-stops (two strings at the same time). This is successful only if they can accurately hear and identify the interval of a perfect fifth. (See Tip 10.) First, make sure your A string is in tune. Play it alone for a long time, letting the pitch settle in your ear. Then play the A and D strings at the same time. If you detect a "wah-wah" sound, you are hearing the sound waves. This means that the strings are close but not quite in tune. If you can't tell if the D is sharp (too high) or flat (too low), experiment by trial and error. If the sound waves disappear and it sounds in tune, double-check it with your tuner or keyboard. The same process can be repeated with the D and G strings, followed by A and E string. Double check the A and E string tuning with A-A-E-E as explained in Tip 10.

On the CD, an A is given as a reference pitch, followed by tuning with double stops. Play each reference pitch alone first, then the double stop. This is for reference only, and not meant to be played "in time" with the recording.

TRACK 2

One of the problems with tuning open fifths ("open," as in open strings) using double stops is that the ear tends to hear chords from the bottom up. Your ear may perceive the D string to be in tune even when you have tuned the A string first. Students need to go slowly. Every player should take enough time to listen and tune carefully, thus improving their ear.

12 MUTES

A mute, placed directly on the bridge, gives a stringed instrument a softer, muffled tone. The most common violin mutes are made of ebony, metal, rubber, or a combination of those materials. Mutes cost from $1.50 to around $5.00. Many violinists keep their mute on the D string close to the tailpiece. The indication in notated music for applying the mute is **con sordino**. **Senza sordino** instructs the player to remove the mute. The very large practice mute almost completely muffles all sound if you need to practice in a hotel or warm up backstage.

From L to R: Metal mute, practice mute, rubber mute (Tourte style)

In the following example, measures 1–4 are played with the mute and measures 6–9 are played without it.

TRACK 3

Use of the mute is more pronounced when used by an entire section of string instruments. Listen to "Nuages" (Clouds) by Claude Debussy, for example, and the soundtrack to Alfred Hitchcock's *Psycho*, by Bernard Herrmann.

13 NATURAL HARMONICS

If you lightly touch (don't press) at the exact halfway point on any string, it will sound an octave higher than the open string. This higher pitch is a natural harmonic. Harmonics sound best with a fast bow stroke. A down-bow starting at the frog can sound very different from an up-bow starting from the tip. For consistency, use the same part of the bow and the same bow direction between notes.

Tuning with Harmonics Tip: To get a good ringing harmonic tone, place your left thumb at the "heel," where the neck meets the back of the violin, and stretch your pinky out over the fingerboard. You may need to fish around with your finger to find the spot where the harmonic really rings. It's exactly at the halfway point on the string. Sometimes just leaning your finger back or forward a bit can help you find the spot. Try this on the A string. Next, bring out your index finger and place it on the D string at a fifth above open D (the pitch A). The same pitch should be produced on the A string with the pinky as on the D string with the index finger. Your left hand is in a location violinists call fourth position. The "0" below index finger and pinky is a reminder that you aren't pressing down on the string, rather just touching the string to produce the ringing harmonic tone. Since use of the same part of the bow will help keep a consistent tone, see Tip 28, Bow Lifts.

```
4 = 1    4 = 1    4 = 1
0   0    0   0    0   0
(A) (D)  (D) (G)  (E) (A)
```

TRACK 4

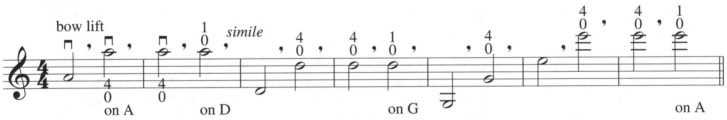

14 ARTIFICIAL HARMONICS VS. NATURAL

Natural harmonics can be found at certain fractional spots on any string (1/2, 1/3, 1/4, and 1/5), such as the halfway point discussed in the previous tip. Artificial harmonics require an additional finger to press down and stop the string. Violinists use the index finger to stop the string, as if fingering a regular note, and lightly add the pinky a perfect fourth above the index finger. Some artificial harmonics require a bigger stretch of the hand, especially on the G string. "Czardas" (1904), by the Italian composer Vittorio Monti, is one of the most famous examples of the use of harmonics in violin solo repertoire. (See Tip 63.)

15 VIOLIN BRANDS

The best violins are handmade by professional luthiers. Although called "violin makers," they often are also builders of violas, cellos, basses, and guitars. Like the renowned Amati family of luthiers, they can often make a great cello as well as a violin. Not everyone can afford or acquire a Stradivarius. Some standard student-level brands of stringed instruments include Meisel, Klaus Mueller, Kroger, Hoffman, Strunal, Glaesel, and Scherl & Roth. Upper-level brands include Eastman, Yuan Qin, and Scott Cao, but there are many more. If you have a favorite violinist, find out what brand they play and check it out. What works for a musician you admire may not be right for you, but it's a starting point.

16 BUYING A VIOLIN (YOU GET WHAT YOU PAY FOR)

If you're looking to purchase a violin, remember this: You get what you pay for. A high-quality instrument will be hand-carved instead of laminated. Laminated instruments are usually glossier in appearance. Although a shiny, new-looking instrument may have more appeal for a young student, most of the best instruments have a flatter, matted finish. A finer violin should have nice flaming (looks like stripes) on the back panel. Ask if the price includes an "outfit" (instrument, bow, case, and possibly some accessories: shoulder rest, rosin, mute, cleaning cloth, spare set of strings, etc.). You will need to use a humidifier in the winter or in dry climates. A humidifier helps prevent the formation of cracks. A crack on a panel is much more serious than a crack in a seam.

Have a knowledgeable player inspect and demonstrate the different instruments for you. If you are a capable player, make sure to play the same exact thing on each instrument, checking its entire range. A new violin will have a bright sound that mellows over time. An older instrument may have an excellent tone, but it will need more maintenance. Find out how old the pegs, bridge, and strings are, and if any work/repair was recently done.

Purfling is the outline on the violin's front and back panels that follows the outer edge. "Real" purfling is different pieces of wood wedged in the panel to protect the instrument. If the edge gets cracked, the purfling can stop the crack from spreading across the panel. The cheaper instruments have painted-on purfling lines instead of inlaid wood ("real") purfling. You can see the paintbrush strokes where the back panel meets the neck or on the corners of the bouts.

Real purfling

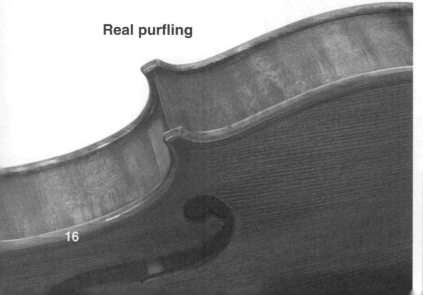

Painted-on purfling

17 CHIN RESTS

Chin rests are very important for the comfort of the jaw and neck, as well as the left arm and collarbone, while playing. Chin rests can be made of plastic, ebony, rosewood, or other materials. Some have a "hump" that goes up over or next to the tailpiece. This is often uncomfortable for younger violinists, depending on the length of the player's neck. The Flesch brand can be ordered with or without a hump. There are also chin rests with gel inside that can better adjust to your chin and jaw shape.

For detailed information on chin rest and shoulder rest fitting, check out this website from the Utrecht School for the Arts in the Netherlands: www.violinistinbalance.nl

Here you will find discussion about the angle, tilt, position, shape, and height – all in the quest for the best setup for comfortable playing.

18 SHOULDER REST, SPONGE, OR NOTHING?

Measure the space between your collar bone and chin: Place your left thumbnail upside-down on your collarbone where the violin would be placed. Reach your index finger up under your chin. Include the width of your finger and thumb by using your right index finger and thumb outside your left-hand fingers. Make sure your head is straight and facing forward.

Compare the length of your neck with the size of your instrument, including chin rest. The extra space can be filled in with a shoulder rest or sponge. Very few professional players use nothing, because they need the support for long days of playing, shifting positions, and using vibrato with a free left hand. Experiment with different sized sponges and adjust where you place your sponge for comfort. Most players secure their sponge to the violin with a large rubber band. Many violin students start with a sponge, and move on to a shoulder rest after a few years of playing.

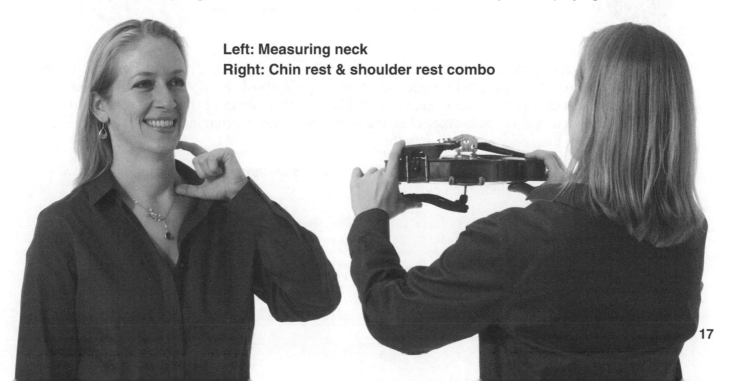

Left: Measuring neck
Right: Chin rest & shoulder rest combo

19 BIG BAD WOLF TONE

The "wolf tone" is an unfortunate sympathetic vibration on one pitch that is common in all instruments of the violin family, although most often the cello. At least, the cellists complain the most! The solution is to purchase a dewolfer (wolf tone eliminator). It's basically a rubber mute that is attached to the string by a small screw similar to the fine tuners.

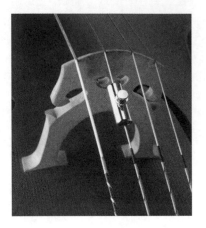

20 GO BACKPACKING!

Young players can easily put on and carry cases with backpack straps. The most practical cases have multiple outer pockets (big enough to hold music/books in a folder), handles, and plenty of room inside for accessories. If you have a pet that sheds, reconsider your violin case covering, because canvas will attract hair and fur. Dependable cases include SKB, Bam, Bobelock, Meisel, Pro Tec, and others. Make sure the nametag on your case has your current contact information.

21 CLEANING AND POLISHING

To avoid rosin buildup and a compromised tone, the violin strings should always be gently scrubbed with a soft clean cloth after every time you play. Wipe fingerprints off the violin surfaces as well. A cloth made of silk or cotton will work quite well. Rubbing alcohol can get serious grit off the string, but be careful not to get a drop of alcohol on the violin finish. Use instrument polish – never furniture polish! – no more than once every six months.

Teaching Tip: If you have students, insist that they have clean hands when playing. Check how often they wash and/or replace their cloth.

22 SITTING POSTURE

Stand whenever possible! There are many good reasons why beginning upper string players stand in their lessons. Standing results in better posture and setup, which gives the player a straighter bow, better tone, etc.

It is not always possible to stand. If you play in an orchestra, you will be sitting most of the time. Proper sitting posture includes sitting on the front half of the chair (unless you are very tall) with both feet flat on the floor, and your back straight. The fingers on both hands should be curved and look relaxed, like you are holding a soft ball. Your wrists should be straight.

Sitting for a long time on the front of your chair will be difficult at first. Take breaks when practicing, and try to "sit tall." Your torso should look as if you are standing. Keep your rib cage up, but try to relax the shoulders.

Teaching Tip: Before students enter for a lesson, hide the chairs, or make or least move them out of the area. Students should get used to standing when playing. Place the cellos in front, and have the upper strings and basses stand behind/next to the cellos.

Practicing Tip: Start out standing, and sit down only if you get tired. Paul Rolland's popular violin method is known for having pupils work on proper balance and motion while playing, starting with the first lesson. See Tip 33 for the "Statue of Liberty," an exercise for beginners that helps develop the left-arm muscles.

23 LEFT-HAND SHAPE

The fingers on the left hand should have a little space between them for a whole step, and should touch together for a half step. Depending on your finger size, you may need to squeeze the fingers together for a half step. Your thumb should be across from your index finger. The knucklebone of the index finger should be across from where the black of the fingerboard meets the brown of the violin neck. See the figure at the right for a close-up view of the left hand.

Most beginners put as many fingers down as possible while playing. For example, when using the third finger (ring finger), their first and second fingers are also down to help hold down the string. If your pinky is too weak to hold down the string on its own, try putting the third finger down with it. Tip 24 has finger strengthening exercises.

Left-hand thumb and knuckle placement, front and back view

Flop all four fingers over the bow stick as if they are very heavy. The thumb should be slightly bent, with its tip on the hill of the frog. Your thumb and second finger may make a closed circle. Then move your pinky up so its tip is resting on top of the bow stick (four fingers flop, pinky on top). Curl the index finger around the stick; many beginners have the bad habit of a straight index finger. Another strategy is to start with a "bunny" shape: second and third finger touch the thumb, while index finger and pinky are in the air like rabbit ears. Try bending the "ears" in the air. This finger strengthening can be practiced with a pen or pencil.

There is more than one tradition with the violin bow hold. The right hand leans more toward the stick in the Russian bow hold. The Franco-Belgian bow hold is more rounded and flexible than the Russian, with a bent pinky. With all players, there are some individual differences, such as wrist height and finger spread.

Teaching Tip: Two Beginner Bow Holds

- Similar to the adult bow hold, but allows students to use larger muscles: Place the thumb under the stick, on the ferrule (metal part). The thumb and bow hair make an L-shape. Many string teachers put a sticker or "pinky nest" on the bow stick so the student/parents can check pinky placement.

- Similar to the adult bow hold, but allows students to work on balancing the bow: Hold the bow the same as the adult hold. The hand is located at the balance point of the bow.

With all bow holds, make sure the thumb is perpendicular to the bow stick. The thumb should be bent a bit, or a lot if you are double-jointed, but never bent backward. Many players develop tension in the right shoulder. When playing on D and G strings, the elbow can be higher, but the shoulder should stay down and relaxed. Since the bow balances on the string, check your bow hold by holding it up toward the ceiling or once the bow is resting on the string.

A. "bunny" shape
B. beginner bow hold with thumb under frog
C. finding the balance point of the bow

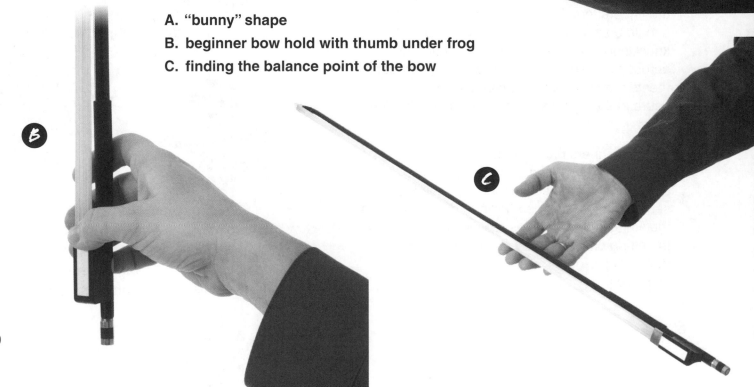

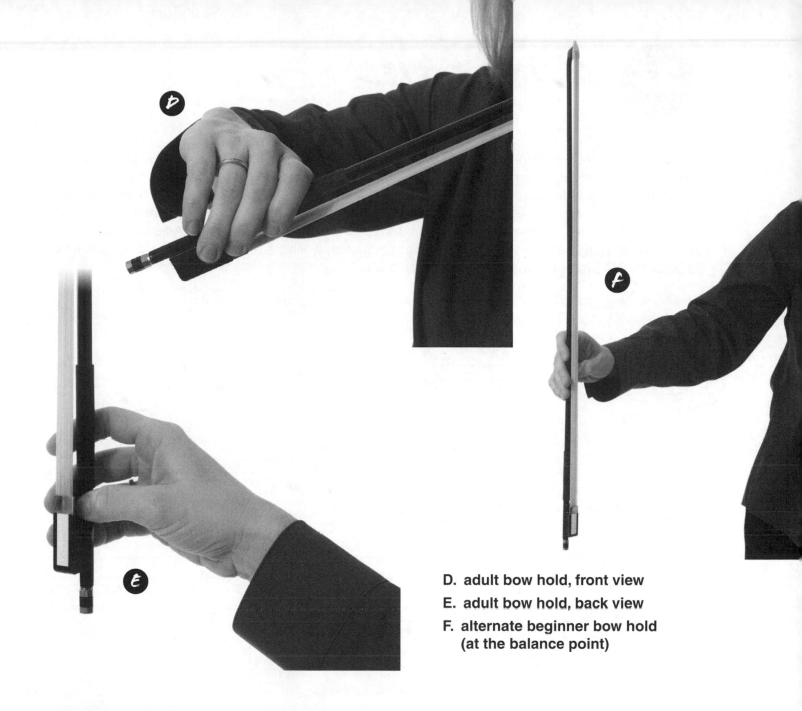

D. adult bow hold, front view

E. adult bow hold, back view

F. alternate beginner bow hold
   (at the balance point)

25 DOWN-BOW, UP-BOW

The down-bow marking (⊓) indicates to pull the bow to the right, usually starting at the frog. The up-bow marking (V) indicates to pull the bow to the left, starting in the upper half of the bow. Since bow markings are confusing when playing on the G string, right and left vs. up in the air and down toward the floor, think about the direction on the E string: down-bow is down in the air, up-bow is up.

Since the frog is the heaviest part of the bow, the down-bow stroke is louder. This is why down-bow is regularly used for notes on the beat, while an up-bow is used for pickup notes. Uniform bowing within a string section helps keep the articulation the same. If you play in a section and don't bother to use the correct bowing, the audience may assume that you are one making the mistakes!

Teaching Tip: If teaching a group, have them practice "shadow bowing" while others are playing. They hold the bow toward the ceiling and move their bows along with the performer's bow direction and rhythm. Have the cellos and basses play a line of music while the violins and violas are shadow bowing.

26 SLURS & TIES

A slur marking is used to indicate when two or more notes are played within the same bow stroke (same bow direction). In music notation, the slur marking is a horizontal arc above or below the notes that are included in the slur. When practicing multiple notes in one bow stroke, begin with just two notes and work your way up to playing string-crossing slurs (between different strings), and then entire scales in one bow stroke, as in the final eight bars of the example below. A tie looks similar to a slur, because it uses the same horizontal arc. However, while a slur incorporates different pitches, a tie connects two or more notes of the same pitch.

TRACK 5

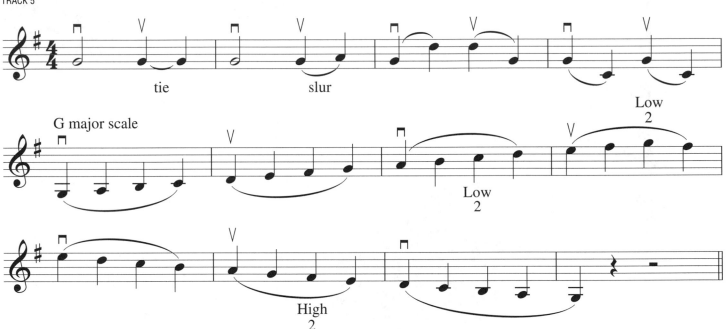

27 CAPTAIN HOOK'S BOWING

A hooked bowing is notated like a slur, but with dots above or below the note heads. It has multiple notes in the same bow direction, like slurs or ties, but stops the bow movement for each note. The result sounds like separate bow strokes. A common use for hooked bowing is to emphasize the downbeat, such as beat one in a minuet or other dance.

Teaching Tip: If you introduce hooks to a young student, make sure they understand that a dot next to the note head (like the dotted half note in measure 8 below) changes the rhythm, while a dot above or below the note head changes only the articulation.

MINUET IN G MAJOR

Christian Petzold

TRACK 6

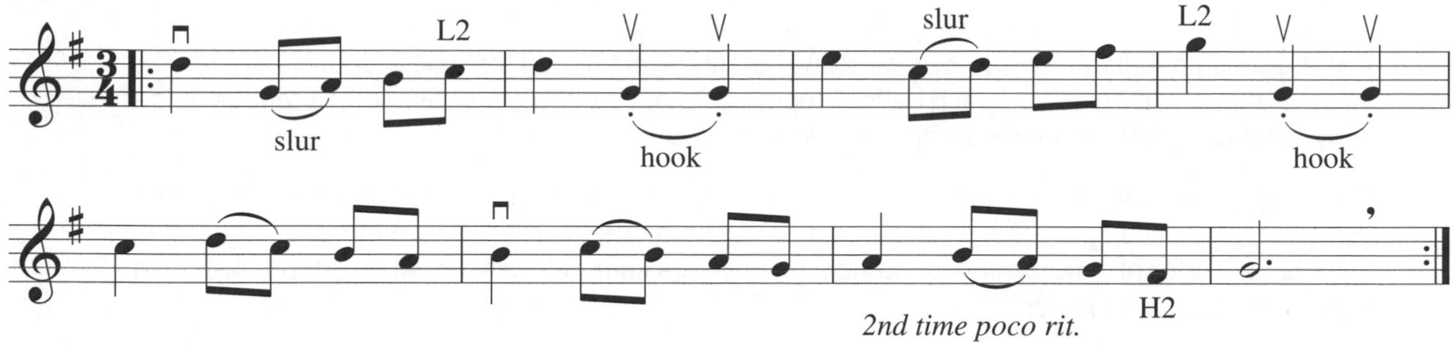

28 BOW LIFTS

A bow lift (') is usually put between two consecutive down-bow markings. The object of a bow lift is to return the bow to its original spot on the string. A bow lift is also called a circle-bow, because the bow literally makes a circle in the air. The bow lift is technically an up-bow in the air, enabling the player to do successive down-bows for a heavy, powerful sound. The symbol for a bow lift is an apostrophe above the music staff. For wind instrument players, the bow lift marking is used as a breath mark. Likewise, string players should feel free to breathe while playing. It fosters excellent communication.

On the third beat of measure 4, lift the bow and make a circle in the air to return it near the frog of the bow on the string. This gets the bow ready for the down-bow in the next measure.

AU CLAIR DE LA LUNE

French Folk Song

TRACK 7

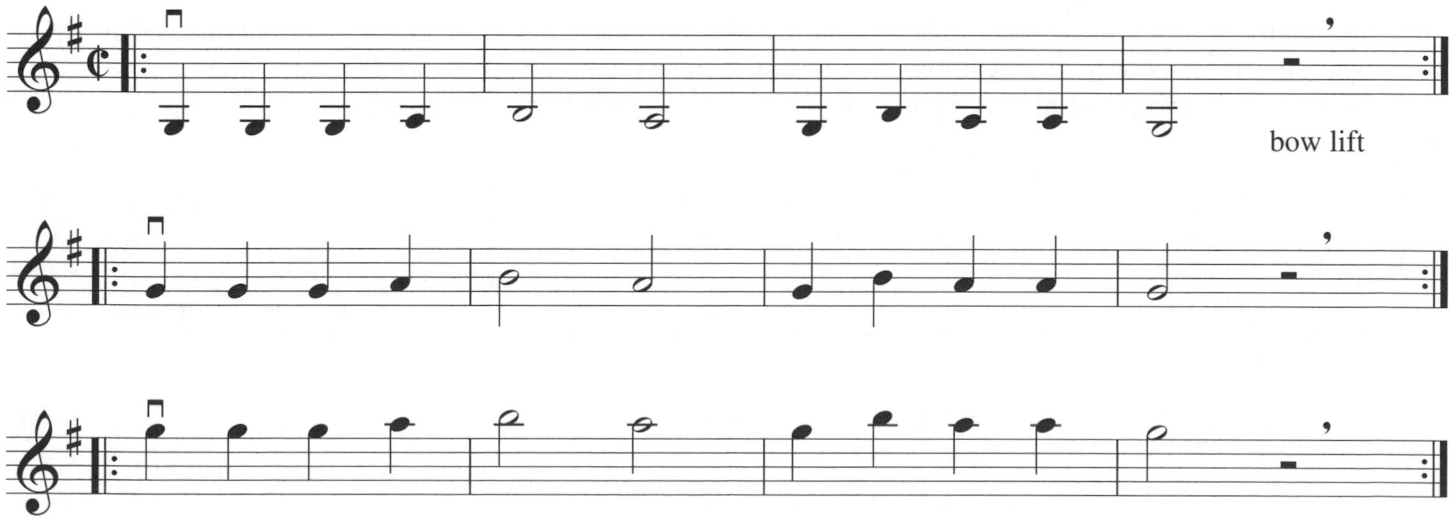

29 PLAYING COL LEGNO

Col legno is an Italian musical term directing string players to use the wood, or stick, of the bow instead of the hair. This is a special-effect sound, one that can be ethereal and mysterious. It is also fairly quiet compared to bowing with the hair of the bow.

Composers also ask players to bounce the stick off the string (*spiccato*: see Tip 31) when playing *col legno*. Unless you play really hard, it should not harm the bow stick. Wipe the stick clean of rosin immediately after playing *col legno*. Some string players keep a less expensive spare bow to use specifically for special effects.

30 SUL PONTICELLO & SUL TASTO

Sul ponticello is an Italian term meaning "at the bridge," indicating a special-effect bowing style. In this technique, the bow is in contact with the strings very close to the bridge; sometimes it can be on top of the bridge. Experiment with how close the bow gets to the bridge to hear the changes in the timbre. Use this technique the next time you want to sound mysterious.

TRACK 8

Sul tasto means to play over the fingerboard, away from the bridge. It facilitates playing at a softer volume without changing bow pressure. *Sul tasto* can also be used for prolonged double stops, because the strings are closer together the further the bow is from the bridge.

TRACK 9

31 BOUNCING THE BOW

Various techniques are used in which the bow is off the string. Find the balance point of your bow, approximately the lower third. This is where it should be placed on the string to begin bouncing, or *spiccato*. Start with the bow on the string, and pull off into the air. Like dribbling a basketball, *spiccato* is easier if you keep it bouncing. *Spiccato* is also known as **sautillé**, **saltando**, or **saltato**. **Jeté** (also called ricochet) is similar to throwing the bow on the string from above, letting it bounce repeatedly in one stroke. Controlling the rebounds is the challenge when using any bouncing technique.

Both "Surprise Symphony Theme" and "Eine kleine Nachtmusik" employ the use of *spiccato* playing. The first ten measures of "Eine kleine Nachtmusik" is a simplified version, without shifts or chords. The second half of the example is the original version.

SURPISE SYMPHONY THEME
Franz Josef Haydn

TRACK 10

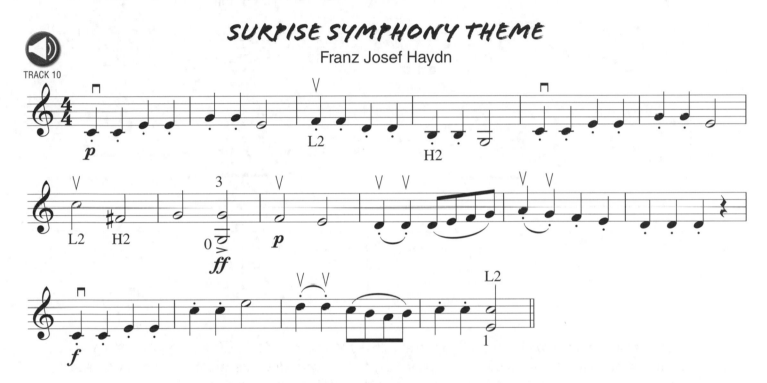

EINE KLEINE NACHTMUSIK
Wolfgang Amadeus Mozart

Internet Assignment: Watch a video of Nikolai Rimsky-Korsakov's *Capriccio Espagnol* (1887). You will hear and see string players use harmonics, vibrato, *pizzicato*, bow lifts, slurs, and hooks. Make note if the violin soloist uses *legato*, *staccato*, *spiccato*, or *jeté* bowing styles.

32 TREMOLO

Tremolo effect is achieved by bowing as fast as possible in very short strokes. The bow can move faster at the tip or upper half of the bow. This sound effect is characteristic of stringed instruments building tension in horror/suspense movie soundtracks. Keep a loose wrist and hand when playing tremolo. Your elbow should be motionless. In notation, *tremolo* is indicated by three short lines or slashes above or below the note head. One or two slashes does not mean tremolo, but can indicate doubled or quadrupled bowing.

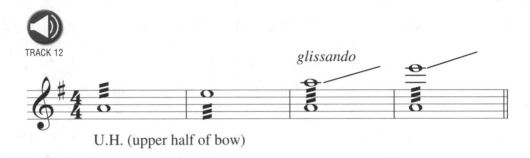

TRACK 12

U.H. (upper half of bow)

33 RELAX!

Violin and viola are called "chin" or "shoulder" instruments, because they are held under the chin and on the left shoulder. Tension often results from having to hold the instrument up and twist the left arm to play. You should be holding it up mostly with your head, so make sure the chin rest and shoulder support are properly sized. (See Tip 18.)

Tapping the thumb against the neck before playing is a good way to check for excess tension. This can be called the "Grape Check" (tap left thumb on the neck and make sure they aren't gripping the neck: If they do, the imaginary grape will get swished). See if you can swing your left elbow. You should be able to do shoulder taps: In playing position, tap the violin's shoulder with your left hand. Next tap the other shoulder.

Teaching Tip: Take a look at Paul Rolland's set of videos called *The Teaching of Action in String Playing*. Rolland's basic premise was to have string students moving, especially in circular motions, while playing. This helps to strengthen the correct muscles, use proper balance, and relieve tension. Many string teachers use exercises that are influenced by Rolland, such as the "Statue of Liberty." The violin is held in the left hand, grasping the shoulder to reinforce rest position, or in fourth position to preview shifting). The arm gets stretched upward, à la Lady Liberty. The violin is then lowered down onto the collarbone/left shoulder from above, resulting in higher placement on the shoulder and better balance. A similar version, which may go over better with older kids, is to have students do the "Nose Check." When they bring their instrument up to playing position, they make sure it goes above their nose before settling on the shoulder. In orchestra rehearsal, have the upper strings do the "Nose Check" while lower strings do the "Grape Check."

34 BEGINNING VIBRATO

Vibrato consists of small, even fluctuations (bends) of the pitch. For string players, the arm, wrist, and/or hand shakes, causing the finger to move while pressing on the string. Violin vibrato is similar to the motion one uses when holding a shaker. Strong fingers are a prerequisite for vibrato. Make sure you are using only one finger of the left hand at a time. Since the third finger and pinky tend to be the weakest, spend time using them alone prior to working on vibrato.

Pre-Vibrato Exercises

1. Finger Strength: In third or fourth position, grab all the way around the violin neck. Keeping the other fingers down (you may need to use the opposite hand to hold down the other fingers), make small independent vibrato motions with each finger.

2. Knuckle Taps: In fourth position, knock lightly with your index or second finger knuckle on the pegs. Be sure to release the tension and move your wrist.

3. Ski Slope: Slide your hand up and down the fingerboard. Try this with harmonics, then pressing down. This sliding sound is called glissando. Slide up the fingerboard with your smallest finger joint bent, then back down with it flat. Next, switch the directions.

4. Put a small Super Ball on the strings. Cover it with your hand and feel how your fingers curve around the ball. Start sliding!

5. Tic-Tacs, box of raisins, or shaker: Find something small that makes a sound and hold it up in your left hand, without the violin. Simulate the vibrato motion and gradually speed it up.

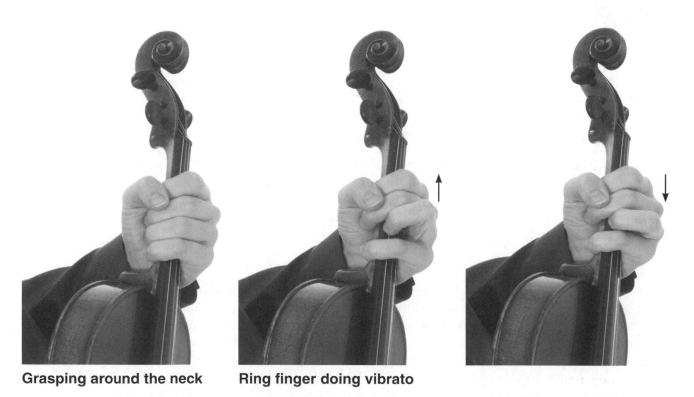

Grasping around the neck   **Ring finger doing vibrato**

Play a fingered note without vibrato. Begin sliding the finger up and down on the string, letting your whole hand move together. Next, put the thumb in place and isolate the finger movement.

Teaching Tip: "Polishing" the string is a quiet exercise that students can do while others are playing for the class. The thumb stays put and a finger moves up and down the string with no right-hand bowing or plucking. This can be done in rest position.

Begin with a very slow, exaggerated vibrato. You can speed it up gradually. If you speed it up too quickly, the vibrato will sound tight and nervous. CD Track 13 plays the same melody twice: first without vibrato, then with a standard or "normal" vibrato. Once you are comfortable with the technique, vibrate immediately when you start most notes.

Many string players have coordination problems when they begin vibrating and bowing. Try playing *pizzicato* (plucking) when using vibrato. Some violinists find it beneficial to take the thumb away from the neck when starting vibrato. A disadvantage of this method is that the player may be able to do vibrato only this way: don't delay putting the thumb back in place. Lightly tapping the thumb against the neck before playing is a good way to check for excess tension.

35 VIBRATO DOS & DON'TS

If you do not play very well in tune, you are not ready for vibrato. Don't try to speed up the vibrato before it feels relaxed. While vibrato is required for music of the Classical and Romantic eras, it is used less in Baroque and Renaissance music. Many contemporary and jazz musicians vary their vibrato speed, or use vibrato as an effect.

When playing a musical passage, try not to use the same vibrato on every note. Use vibrato differently according to the phrasing, varying its use so you don't sound too mechanical. Some notes may be affected by a faster, deeper vibrato, while other notes use only a lighter vibrato toward the end of their duration. Try this: Begin a phrase with light vibrato. With each successive note, allow the vibrato to get faster into the middle of the phrase, to develop its shape. As the phrase nears its end, let the vibrato back off gradually. Listen to different gospel and blues singers to compare their vibrato use.

Experiment with starting a note without vibrato, and gradually add in a slow vibrato on the second note in CD Track 14. This is called "warming it up." You can also try speeding up the vibrato gradually, and then slowing it down gradually, all over the course of one long note. Many players use varying vibrato speeds and degrees of vibrato as techniques of expression to suit different types of music.

TRACK 14

36 PLAYING IN TUNE: KNOW YOUR INTERVALS

Intervals are the space between two different pitches. For example, the violin is tuned in perfect fifths. If you play open G-G-D-D, it should sound like the beginning of "Twinkle, Twinkle, Little Star." The proper placement of the first (index) finger can be tested on the D string in this manner.

TRACK 15

The proper placement of the third finger on any string can be checked with open A followed by third finger, which should sound like Wagner's "Bridal Chorus" ("Here Comes the Bride"). Try this starting on all the open strings. This interval is called a perfect fourth.

The interval of an octave (also called perfect octave) is between one pitch and another at half or double its frequency. It is the top and bottom note of major and minor scales. "(Somewhere) Over the Rainbow" from *The Wizard of Oz* begins with an ascending octave.

Get the pinky in tune! Try Beethoven's "Ode to Joy" with open A, then with pinky (the whole melody on the D string). Now transpose this melody and play it on E, then A, then G. Be aware that most inexperienced violinists tend to play with a flat pinky.

ODE TO JOY
Ludwig van Beethoven

TRACK 16

37 THE PHYSICS OF PLAYING IN TUNE

Playing in tune is a combination of knowing what the sound should be before playing, responding, and knowing the tendency of your instrument and your own physicality. In other words, listen and adjust.

Sympathetic vibration, also called "ringing tone," occurs when a string vibrates its note name, even in a different octave. For example, if you play a G on the D string, your open G will vibrate if your finger is in the right spot. Play a D on the A string, and your D should vibrate. Every E, A, D, and G on the violin, when fingered, should cause this ringing tone on the corresponding open string. However, the vibration is easiest to see on the lower strings and most difficult to see on the higher strings. This is because the lower strings have a thicker gauge. Sympathetic vibrations can be beneficial to playing in tune, especially with the third and fourth fingers.

Use this method for checking intonation when you start shifting: For example, in third position on the A string, your first finger should make the open D vibrate. For more on shifting, see Tip 39.

If you know what pitch to expect before pulling the bow, you will be able to adjust faster to get it in tune. The best players make immediate adjustments because they are listening and know the piece. They are able to hear the pitch in their head before they play it. Listen to recordings of pieces you are learning; it will help develop your ear.

Be aware of your left-hand shape and placement. The thumbs often cause problems in both hands. Before playing or after rests, always check both thumbs. Make sure the left thumb is across from your index finger, and that the largest knuckle of your index finger is where the black and brown meet on your violin neck.

38 SCALES ARE LIKE VEGETABLES

Although scales and etudes (technical studies) may be a musician's least favorite to practice, they are good for your playing. The Carl Flesch scale exercises are widely regarded among violinists for establishing a good fingering system. Scales make your fingers and ears more familiar with different modes and keys. Scale passages are common in music and can be practiced with different rhythms for variety. It is more practical to spend your time learning scales well in one octave at a time rather than being able to run up and down your violin in three octaves at once, because scale passages in music are rarely more than one octave. To be a versatile player, work on major, natural minor, melodic minor, and harmonic minor scales, as well as the blues scale.

TRACK 17

31

CAN-CAN

from *Orpheus in the Underworld*
Jacques Offenbach

TRACK 18

Allegro con moto

You may already be familiar with some of the different modes. For example, the **Ionian mode** is the same as the major scale, and the **Aeolian** is the same as the natural minor scale. To learn different modes starting on any pitch, reference the whole- and half-step sequences listed below: **Dorian**, **Phrygian**, **Lydian**, **Mixolydian**, **Aeolian**, and **Locrian**.

Mode	Whole (W) and Half Steps (h) in ascending order						
Ionian	W	W	h	W	W	W	h
Dorian	W	h	W	W	W	h	W
Phrygian	h	W	W	W	h	W	W
Lydian	W	W	W	h	W	W	h
Mixolydian	W	W	h	W	W	h	W
Aeolian	W	h	W	W	h	W	W
Locrian	h	W	W	h	W	W	W

These modes are useful for improvisation. Consult a jazz text (or player) on the use of scales and modes in improvisation.

39 SLIDE, DON'T JUMP

Shifting on the violin can be difficult, because going higher on the fingerboard is unfamiliar, and because and shifting back and forth in positions impacts the balance and muscles in your arm and hand. The advantage of shifting higher for violinists and violists is that your hand moves closer to your face and you get a better view of your fingers.

When shifting, keep your thumb moving lightly along with your left hand as one unit. Some players slide a finger up the fingerboard then quickly add the finger to be used for the ultimate pitch at the very end of the shift. For example, if your need to shift on the E string from G in first position to the G an octave higher, shift your hand to the needed position, play the D with the first finger, and add the fourth finger, which is ready for the G. Most of the mistakes in shifting result from not hearing the pitch ahead of time, and physically not shifting far enough, producing a flat pitch. A certain fear is present when you can't hear the pitch ahead of time, so you may end up playing a guessing game, reaching up into unfamiliar territory. This fear/stress can often result in a weak tone, which only adds to the possible intonation problem. To overcome this when shifting, remember to listen, breathe, and stay strong with the bow.

TRACK 19

(on A)   (on E)

Plan Ahead
Where will your hand and elbow end up after the shift? Lighten the weight of your hand just before shifting. Try a sliding shift, in which you glissando (slide) up or down between the two notes. When figuring out when to shift in a piece, try not to shift three notes in a row, or use the same finger three times. If a difficult shift is giving you trouble, try playing it backward, up or down an octave, etc. very slowly. Close your eyes to make sure you are really listening.

40 PIZZICATO

The Italian term **pizzicato** (abbreviated *pizz.*) instructs the player to pluck the string with the right hand. The traditional classical *pizzicato* style is to draw the sound out of the string in an upward motion.

For long *pizzicato* endurance, many players alternate between the first and second fingers of the right hand. (The index finger is the most common.) For more volume, use the first and second fingers together like one big finger.

The next example shows a violin duet for the tune "Dance of the Hours" from Amilcare Ponchielli's opera *La Gioconda* (1876). Both violinists play *pizzicato*.

TRACK 20

DANCE OF THE HOURS

from *La Gioconda*
Amilcare Ponchielli

The following features the jazz-style *pizz.* and shows how a violinist can play in a walking-bass fashion, much like an upright bass player. Try using the side of your finger and as much flesh as possible.

TRACK 21

LEFT-HAND PIZZICATO

Left-hand *pizzicato* is sometimes a necessity if there is not enough time to switch from *arco*. It works well if the last *pizzicato* note is an open string. It is also used as a special effect in between *arco* notes, to show off the player's virtuosity, such as in Nicolò Paganini's "Caprice No. 24" (c. 1805). Left-hand *pizzicato* is most often done with the pinky. In the following example, "+" signs are used to indicate *pizzicato*.

TRACK 22

BARTÓK PIZZICATO

Also called a **snap *pizzicato***, the **Bartók *pizzicato*** has a history with Hungarian composer Béla Bartók (1881–1945), whose writing was influenced by the folk music of his native land. The snap *pizz.* is indicated in music with a sign above the note, as shown in the example below. It is often accompanied by a *sforzando* marking, a directive to perform the note with strong emphasis. It is accomplished by plucking the string high off the fingerboard, hard enough to make it snap back. While it does not harm the instrument, repeated snap *pizz.* can pull the string out of tune. For more about this amazing composer, read *The Music of Béla Bartók* by Elliott Antokoletz (University of California Press, 1984).

TRACK 23

This percussive sound is also particularly striking when an entire string section does it. The Bartók pizz. is common in contemporary classical music and movie soundtracks.

43 STRUMMING CHORDS

Some violinists play chords with their fingers – or, in rare cases – with a guitar pick. Use a hard pick, with the violin in guitar (rest) position. Players most often pluck chords with their thumb from the bottom up. Because the violin is fretless, playing chords well in tune can be problematic. Try strumming only two of the pitches, and get them in tune before adding the third, then fourth, pitch.

TRACK 24

44 ALTERNATIVE STYLES

The world of alternative string playing has been expanding into folk, jazz, rock, and world music. Although the guitar has been used in a variety of genres for a long time, the violin is catching up. Ensembles like the Turtle Island String Quartet, Kronos Quartet, Hampton String Quartet, and Vitamin String Quartet have helped change the image of the violin. Pioneering violinists in the jazz style include Stéphane Grappelli, Joe Venuti, Mark O'Connor, Darol Anger, Randy Sabien, Julie Lyonn Lieberman, and many more. Don't limit yourself only to classical music on the violin. The violin can play anything!

For fiddle violin styles, see Tip 55. For the violin in the rock genre, see Tip 49.

Check out the nontraditional players' websites listed in Tip 101.

45 ELECTRIFY YOUR ACOUSTIC VIOLIN

Besides playing an electric violin, you can amplify your acoustic violin by attaching a pickup. Most acoustic pickups are fastened at the tailpiece with a cord that runs to the bridge. It attaches to the bridge with a small piece of copper. Some pickups attach to the fingerboard. Many have the standard quarter-inch jack. With a cable and pickup, you can plug into an amp and be as loud as any electric guitar. The jazz/blues violinist Stuff Smith was one of the first players to amplify his instrument.

Preamps

Unless you enjoy the harsh bow sounds amplified from the pickup, usually attached to the bridge, you need to use a preamp. Without a preamp, the tone in the upper range will sound very thin, and bow sounds are often too loud in the balance. Pick a preamp that has EQ options such as bass, treble, mid, and brilliance. Many companies that produce pickups also make a matching preamp. Fishman and Realist are the best-known pickup manufacturers. The Realist pickup is installed underneath one of the bridge feet. It has an excellent tone. You will probably need an extra cable (patch cord) and a 9-volt battery for the preamp. They are worth the hassle if you want a better amplified sound. Most electric violins include an internal preamp. Some purists prefer to amplify their sound with a microphone, either mounted on the instrument or on a stand. Since the bass has less mobility onstage, jazz bass players have often used this method.

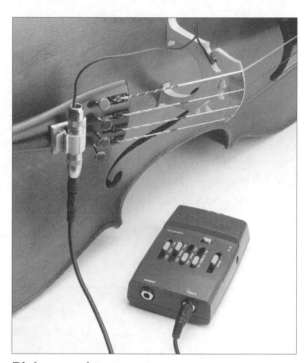

Pickup and preamp

Electric violins first became available in the 1930s, although they were more common in the 1950s when Fender began production. Since the 1990s, the electric violin has gained popularity in almost every genre of music, especially with its live performance capabilities.

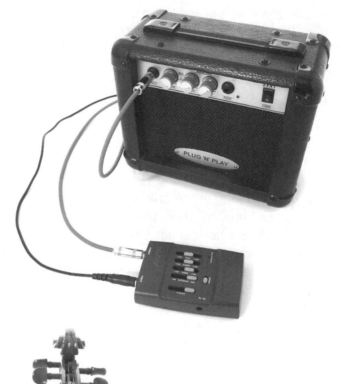

Electric Violin Shopping Tip: There are many options for brands of electric violins. Like purchasing an acoustic, playing before you buy is important. Electric violin makers include Fender, NS Design, Starfish Designs, Vector, Violectra, Wood Violins, Shar, Yamaha, Zeta, and more. Many electric violins have MIDI (Musical Instrument Digital Interface) inputs for recording, a headphone jack for silent practice, and the capability to play along with a CD player/iPad/iPod. Some music stores will let you try out violins in a practice room with an amp, or take it home for a few days before purchasing. Get the return policy in writing from the company before you buy their violin. You can also shop online for electric violins, pickups, preamps, and amps for acoustic or electric violins.

47 WHERE'S MY VIOLIN AMP?

Amplifier choice is very important. Unfortunately, most electric violins don't come with their own custom amp. And if they do, it might not be very good quality. Remember, you get what you pay for. The violin has a similar range as the guitar, but a keyboard amp may sound better with your electric violin, especially in its lower range. Turn the treble down and the bass level up to avoid that nasty, tinny sound. Before purchasing an amp that sounds great at half volume, you need to test it at your performance volume.

Another important aspect to consider in choosing an amp is whether you'll be using it with an acoustic violin, with a pickup or microphone, or solely an electric. Acoustic instruments can feed back easily when the amp is turned up loud, especially if you are using a standard keyboard or guitar amp. There are special amps made for acoustic instruments that are designed to minimize feedback. The electric violin does not have this problem, but you may need to use the same amp for different performance settings. An acoustic instrument with a microphone or pickup is typically chosen more often for a smaller venue. Once again, test all performance volumes before you take it home.

48 HEARING YOURSELF ONSTAGE

The sounds you hear from your instrument, and how you hear other instruments around you, can be very different when playing in a cozy recital hall compared to a large concert hall, outdoor festival, or that local dive bar where you get your first rock gig. Your sound could be completely obliterated by a drum set or electric bass in any of these settings. There are many balance issues to consider, especially if your group also has guitar, keyboards, a horn section, etc. Always try to get in some playing time in whatever venue you'll be performing before the gig itself. At least start and stop each tune if there isn't enough time for a complete run-through.

Many violinists suffer some loss of hearing in their left ear. This occurs even with classical players, so if you are doing jazz and rock, be especially careful. When a jazz combo or rock band performs, many players use earplugs. This is because these smart musicians plan on being able to hear for many years. Earplugs also help filter out excess background noise, and help you hear the music better in loud rock concert settings. Many performers use **in-ear monitors**. They work like earplugs and an onstage monitor together. As they become more common, demand for the product makes them more affordable. Make sure you have used them in several rehearsals before using them in concert.

Keep in mind that rock concerts get louder as the night goes on. The best sound quality is not in the front row. The sound station is usually in the middle of the audience, where you can hear the best mix.

Healthy Hearing Tip: If you are listening with headphones, including ear buds, and someone else can hear the music a few feet away, it's too loud. Even if it doesn't bother your ears now, long-term exposure can also cause irreparable hearing damage. If you are in a concert and music makes your ears feel warm or there is some ringing after, it was too loud. Keep a few pairs of earplugs in your car and in your desk at work. Keep a pair in your instrument case as well.

49 THE VIOLIN IN ROCK AND JAZZ

The history of the violin in jazz predates its place in rock. Joe Venuti, Eddie South, Stuff Smith, and Stéphane Grappelli are known as the jazz violin pioneers. Players who have helped redefine the violinist's role include Mark Wood, Jerry Goodman (jazz/rock, fusion, progressive rock), Nigel Kennedy (many genres), Charlie Daniels (country rock), Stéphane Grappelli (jazz), Joe Venuti (jazz), Randy Sabien (jazz), Julie Lyonn Lieberman (jazz/alternative styles), Mark O'Connor (many genres), Regina Carter (jazz, pop, R&B, and more), Darol Anger (bluegrass, classical, folk, jazz), and others.

Many rock groups since the 1970s use the violin as a regular member of the band. The genre of Violin Rock appears on various music websites. Rock groups that use the violin as a regular instrument include Kansas (Robbie Steinhardt and David Ragsdale), UK (Eddie Dobson), Trans-Siberian Orchestra, ELO, Dexys Midnight Runners (now called Dexys), Dave Matthews Band, Boud Deun, Judgement Day, Quark Quintet, and more.

50 THE VIOLIN AS LEAD VS. RHYTHM

Your role in the ensemble can be defined by your group's instrumentation. Sometimes the violinist functions as the lead guitar or vocal part, playing the melody or a solo. More often, the violin plays a countermelody, or plays a more rhythmic role. Check out Boyd Tinsley, the violinist in the Dave Matthews Band. He covers many roles, often playing background pizz. chords or a quiet countermelody, but at other times he has an exposed solo.

Listen to what the rhythm guitar does in most rock bands. The violin can cover the same part, whether bowing or strumming chords. If you are doing a cover of a tune, you need to be aware of the range of your instrument. You can cover rhythm guitar, keyboard (right hand, not the bass line), or voice.

51 MOVE WHEN YOU PLAY

Violin playing is very hard on the human body, especially the parts that aren't moving. The shoulders often pull too far forward, neck and back problems can develop, tendonitis can form, and the left elbow can get acquire symptoms similar to tennis elbow. Move along with the music, using your natural playing motions. It helps enhance your performance, and encourages oxygen to get to your muscles. (Think blood flow.) Watch the best players and decide what works best for your playing.

Nadja Salerno-Sonnenberg and Joshua Bell are well-known classical violinists who move around a lot when they play. This is true of many violinists. It can make a performance more interesting, and can help you relax and relieve tension while playing. You may ask, "Why should I move if I'm not a rock player or soloist?" Review Tip 33.

52 EFFECTS PROCESSORS

DigiTech and Griffin Effects are well-known companies that make dependable effects processors. Make sure the device you purchase includes foot switches, volume control, effect buttons capable of editing, drum machine, expression pedal for real-time adjustment, LED display (so you can see in a dark venue), inputs and outputs, headphone jack, AC power supply, tuner, etc. Some processors require a 9-volt battery, even with a power supply, so keep a supply of spare batteries as well.

Take your electric violin, or acoustic with the pickup, to a music store that has a guitar department and try out pedals and effect (stomp) boxes. Guitar effects processors will work fine for your violin; just remember an extra cable/patch cord.

Track 23 demonstrates a violin with a **distortion** effect. Distortion is also called **overdrive**.

TRACK 25

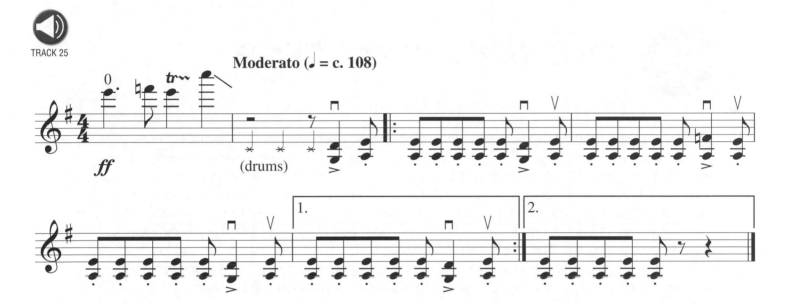

If you add distortion to your sound, the effect makes the articulation somewhat muddy. To achieve the same-sounding length as your clean/untreated sound, your bow articulations must be shorter. This is similar to the orchestral (ensemble) staccato being shorter than the execution of solo *staccato*. Work for a great *spiccato* and *staccato*, and your distorted sounds will be as well-articulated as your clean sound. An electric violinist can imitate the different effects that guitar players use with a pick or fingers, but can also use the bow for endless possibilities.

Other popular effects include **chorus** and **delay**. Delay is a kind of repeating echo, which can be compared to a "ping-pong" echo. Chorus effect results in a big stereo sound. It is often achieved by slightly detuning the original signal in one channel compared to the other. Each channel can be panned far right and far left to increase the "bigness" of the sound.

You've been hearing reverb on every track of the CD. This effect puts your sound in a room so it does not sound dry. Reverbs can range from small rooms to concert hall to parking garages. If you listen carefully to Track 26, you can hear the echo of the performing space, programmed to simulate different room sizes. The following Mozart excerpt is played three times. The first example demonstrates a **small room**; the second a **medium hall**; and the third a very **large hall**.

AVE VERUM CORPUS
Wolfgang Amadeus Mozart

53 THE SUZUKI METHOD

Shinichi Suzuki (1898–1998) was one of the best-known violin teachers in history. He emphasized parent involvement in students' lessons and music education, including parents attending their child's lessons, monitoring practice, and listening to recordings of pieces being learned. Students often start Suzuki violin lessons as young as three years old. For Suzuki resources, go to https://suzukiassociation.org. Playing in tune and with an excellent tone were of highest priority. The Suzuki method books feature "tonalizations," in which the student plays long tones and learns about unisons, harmonics, etc. The books also have basic fingerings, even in the third and fourth books. Most traditional method books do not include as many fingerings and place a higher emphasis on reading standard music notation. Check out Tip 85 for more about playing by ear.

54 INSTRUMENT SUBSTITUTE

The sound of the violin is often compared to the human voice. Both have many options for expression, such as slides, scoops, changes in timbre, and use of vibrato. There are also percussive effects with the violin. The hollow body of the instrument can be gently knocked, while the bridge can be lightly played with pencils. The violin is so versatile; its only limits are technique and imagination.

The violin can function as the guitar of a rock band. Check out Mark Wood's recordings, in which his violin often sounds just like a guitar. In addition to designing instruments, composing, and performing, he has also done clinics with school orchestras in which they play rock songs. His website is markwoodmusic.com.

55 COUNTRY-STYLE FIDDLE LICKS

What's the difference between a violin and a fiddle? The player and the music itself. The same player can employ many different styles on the same instrument. Although this can be true, players often use a lower bridge for fiddle playing to ease the execution of chords. Check out the fiddle styles of Benny Thomasson, Mark O'Connor, Byron Berline, Sam Bush, et al. Sometimes fiddlers retune their instrument to A-E-A-E, in which the bottom two strings are a whole step higher. This alternate tuning is done so that chords can be played more easily.

Fiddle-style playing has a distinct use of the bow. There are many open strings and double stops. "Chopping" is playing at the frog, using small bow strokes (often consecutive down-bows) on the off-beats. Fiddle players typically use a looser bow (less tightening of the adjusting screw) than classical, and often use less pressure and vibrato. The upper half of the bow is commonly used for fast runs.

The rendition of the American folksong "Bile Them Cabbage Down" on Track 27 demonstrates some basic fiddle techniques. In addition to the double stops as notated in the printed music, listen to the other parts playing the off-beat chops as well as the break (more difficult line).

TRACK 27

BILE THEM CABBAGE DOWN
North American Fiddle Tune

43

56 BLUEGRASS & COUNTRY MUSIC

Country music bands usually include a violin playing in a fiddle style, vocals, guitar, bass, drumset, and keyboards. Check out Louise Mandrell, the Dixie Chicks, Taylor Swift, and Shania Twain.

Bluegrass groups customarily feature a fiddle, mandolin, banjo, guitar, bass, high vocal harmonies, and sometimes a drumset. Both bluegrass and country music are conventionally diatonic, but bluegrass tends to be more consistently upbeat and instrumental. Bluegrass often uses the lowered seventh scale degree, also called a blue note. For more information on bluegrass, check out *Bluegrass for Beginners* by Robert Amchin.

57 FOLK INFLUENCES

Many kinds of music have direct folk influences, and many violinists have expanded their instrument across different cultures. Phil Beer, Samson Kehimkar, James "Chick" Stripling, and Paddy Le Mercier are known for extending the violin into folk styles. For Celtic fiddle work, check out Randal Bays, Kevin Burke, Brian Conway, Matt Cranitch, Frankie Gavin, Andy McGann, Martin Hayes, Eileen Ivers, Tommy Peoples, Gerry O'Connor, Paul O'Shaughnessy, Bridget Regan, Marie Reilly, and Brendan Mulvihill. Groups such as Cruachan, Primordial, Skyclad, and Horslips are known for playing Celtic metal, while the Dropkick Murphys and Flogging Molly usually play Celtic punk.

Folk playing often utilizes extremes of the bow: the upper half for fast playing with many string crossings, and close to the frog for heavy accents and chopping. The "Scottish snap" has a stress or accent on the first note. It is a 16th note followed by a dotted eighth note, and is usually played in the lower half of the bow.

58 CHOPPING

The chop sound is used most often in fiddle styles. It is a percussive sound similar to snare drum hits on the offbeats. The proper technique involves dropping the bow on the string near the frog, often with consecutive down-bows. It can be done with a single pitch or with chords. Bluegrass fiddler Richard Greene is acknowledged as the inventor of the chop, while Darol Anger is generally credited with popularizing the technique. Do an Internet search to find out more about both these gentlemen.

Listen again to CD Track 27, "Bile Them Cabbage Down," introduced in Tip 55. Note the chords chopping in the backup part.

59 PITCH BENDS & GRACE NOTES

The Italian term *glissando* indicates that the player should slide between two different pitches. Sliding between pitches (**pitch bend**) is more common in alternative styles (rock, jazz, fiddle, and folk) than in classical styles. The bend, also called a scoop or swoop, is often used going up to a note from a half step or less. Another option is a **fall**, descending at the end of a note.

Grace notes are added as an ornament in Baroque, folk, and jazz styles. A grace note is usually played as a 16th note or faster, slurred into the following note. It can be from above or below the next note. In music notation, the grace note is much smaller in font size from the other notes, and often has a slash through the note stem.

TRACK 28

GAVOTTE
François-Joseph Gossec

60 IMPROVISATION MADE EASY

Improvisation can at first seem intimidating for beginners, especially if you are used to reading music. One way to begin is with just one pitch: Find all the ways you can change the tone quality, and improvise different rhythms. Gradually add a few more notes. The pentatonic scale (black keys on the piano) is only five pitches, but also works well. Improvising over a drone, a long-held note in the bass range, can sound very cool. Practicing scales, including the modes, and arpeggios will help you know your way around the fingerboard and will aid in fluid improvisation. If you play a note that sounds wrong, slide away from that pitch to something that sounds better.

You don't have to be able to follow fast chord changes to be able to improvise. However, knowing the key you are in and the basic chord progression that your style of music follows is invaluable. In the majority of Western music, the primary chords in any given key often use the following pattern: I–IV–V7. While jazz chords are usually extended further, the I–IV–V chords are used in everything from the blues to Mozart to contemporary pop and rock tunes.

45

61 SPECIAL EFFECTS WITH ACOUSTIC

You do not need an effects processor to make wild sounds on the violin. Explore the different timbres available with *glissando* (sliding the left hand up or down the string), or a harmonic *glissando* (sliding but not pressing the finger down, so that various harmonics sound). Take techniques you already know and combine them. For example, once you are confident with harmonics, combine them with *glissando*, *sul ponticello*, *pizzicato*, etc.

CD Track 29 demonstrates a normal *gliss.* first, contrasted with a harmonic *gliss.* Both are on the D string.

TRACK 29

62 SCARY SOUNDS

Hold your bow in a fist like an angry cave man. Next drag the bow across the string as slowly as possible. This sounds similar to a door slowly creaking. Try some high double stops with heavy consecutive down-bows at the frog.

TRACK 30

Have a go at using something other than your bow on the strings. Pencils are a cheap option; just don't drop one into your violin. More interesting sound effects can be made by bowing below the bridge, plucking behind the nut, lightly knocking on one of the panels, etc. The basic GarageBand software or app will allow you to record something similar to a horror film soundtrack. You can have a great result with multiple tracks layered together, as in CD Track 31.

TRACK 31

33 CHORDS (TRIPLE & QUADRUPLE STOPS)

Triple and quadruple stops are almost always played on stringed instruments from the bottom up. Bow the bottom two notes together and use the rest of the bow (more than half) to play the top two notes immediately after. Use the whole bow with plenty of vibrato. If you are plucking, strum the strings evenly from the bottom note up, like a guitarist or pianist.

CD Track 32 features chords from Monti's "Czardas." (See Tip 14.)

CZARDAS
Vittorio Monti

TRACK 32

64 SIGHT-READING

Professional and amateur orchestra members often sight-read (without seeing the part in advance) in rehearsals. Players also sight-read something on a gig; a request is made and your group has the sheet music, but you've never played it before. Studio musicians are expert sight-readers, because every additional hour in the studio results in an increase in the fee.

Sight-Reading Tip: Concentrate on rhythm. Don't stop. Don't worry as much about proper fingerings or missed bowings. Instead, try to get most of the right notes and the gist of the piece. Graduates of the school of "faking it" know how to look ahead in the music. Pick a realistic tempo after glancing at the most difficult sections. It is better to play the piece slowly but at a steady tempo. And remember, don't stop.

If you are sight-reading in an ensemble, ask ahead of time if you are playing it "as written," which means with all repeats. Check to see if there is a D.C. al Fine (repeat back to the beginning and go through until the end/Fine) or a D.S. al Fine (repeat back to the sign and go through until the end/Fine). If you are sight-reading a fairly easy piece, put in all the articulations and dynamics.

65 HOW TO FAKE IT

Every musician has gotten lost in the music, but the professionals don't let the audience know. For example, what if your music stand blows over during an outdoor wedding processional? The bridal party is coming toward your string quartet, and as the first violinist you need to provide the melody for a selection from Handel's *Water Music*. Fortunately, you are a consummate professional, and are aware of the key, form, and chord progression. You have the skills to play this familiar melody by ear.

If you are running a rehearsal and the group is losing its way, call out the next rehearsal number or the next counting that may be helpful for a section. Large cues at new phrases and saying "now" can help get a group back together. Always be aware of the road map of the piece. Is there a key change or a meter change? The recapitulation (return of the beginning theme) is easy to recognize, so mark it in the music. If rehearsal time is limited, get the music ahead of time and make any necessary markings.

Teaching Tip: Prior to sight-reading, having students count, sing, or clap rhythms. Pointing out when sections are together (or apart) can save rehearsal time on a new piece. While listening to a piece prior to playing it can help students play a piece together and better in tune, it will not help their reading.

66 TROUBLE READING TREBLE?

Many players already know how to read treble clef from playing piano (the right hand), flute, clarinet, trumpet, recorder, or from general music classes back in primary school. The treble clef is also called the G clef, because the swirl in the clef sign circles around the note G on the music staff. An oft-used mnemonic device to remember ascending treble clef lines is "Every Good Boy Does Fine;" the spaces can be remembered as F-A-C-E. Reading the treble clef lines and spaces becomes more difficult when you encounter notes in the extreme high or low ranges. Ledger lines extend above the staff for high notes, and below the staff for lower notes. The low G string on the violin is below the second ledger line under the staff.

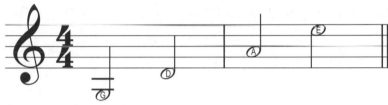

67 HEAD BANGING (IT'S NOT JUST FOR METAL)

Knowing how to cue is very important when playing in a chamber ensemble that does not have a conductor. This body language is also valuable for a section leader within a large orchestra. Violin and viola players can cue with their scroll, so go wild! Make it very clear: up for an upbeat, and down for a downbeat. We string players can also use our bows very dramatically, as long as we don't hit anyone.

Unlike wind players, string players don't need to breathe to make the instrument speak. However, string players use inhalation to indicate cues and phrasing. Breathing in as a preparation to start a piece is much more professional than counting off. For more information about cues, take a conducting course or read a book about conducting. The best players know what conductors know about communication. Check out *Conducting Technique* by Brock McElheran (Oxford University Press) or *The Modern Conductor* by Elizabeth A. H. Green (Prentice Hall).

Alternative Ensemble Communication Tip

Plan who is cueing a certain section, and make sure you can see that person in performance and recording situations, as well as in rehearsal. Many groups have a regular setup for rehearsal, which changes a bit for a performance in front of an audience. This can be drastically compromised if you are the opening act for a stage-hogging headliner band. Your group may also have to do a different setup when recording in a studio. Try to find out how the setup will have to change ahead of time; for example, the drummer is usually in his/her own room.

68 IN THE STUDIO

If you are recording with an acoustic violin, try to record with a sound engineer who has experience recording classical music. The violin sounds great on a hardwood floor or in a room that has had acoustical treatment. More than one microphone, and the quality of the mic, is very important. Have at least two mics, one above the bridge and another toward, but not too close to, the bridge. Before recording, warm up in your full range, move as you normally do when playing, and make sure you have plenty of space for your bow in all directions.

If recording with an electric violin, tell the recording engineer to treat the instrument like an electric guitar. Since the signal is direct, you don't have to worry about mic placement, just extra batteries and headphones.

Bring a violinist – or at least a musician familiar with the music – along with you to the studio. This person can sit in the sound room with the engineer to give you feedback. When in doubt, record an extra take; it is well worth the time and investment rather than having to go back into the studio and rerecord. Take the time to hear everything you recorded played back. Point out any background/extraneous sounds. Feel free to ask a lot of questions, especially if you are new to recording.

69 ORCHESTRAL REHEARSAL TIPS

In an orchestral setting, be mindful of proper rehearsal etiquette. The dependable players have well-marked parts; always have a pencil. Violinists can talk, chew gum, and even eat while playing. Refrain from all of these behaviors, because it can irritate the wind players – or worse, the conductor.

If you are in rehearsal and have a question about a possible misprint in your part, wait until a break and ask the conductor if you can check something in his score. Parts often have misprints, but it should be correct(ed) in the score. If you are the section leader (principal), one of your responsibilities is to communicate any changes to your section. Another part of the principal's job is to be aware of the other string sections' bowings, and even the wind players' articulations, if you share a line in the music.

Section Member's Tip

If you are a "section" violinist, you are not the principal player. You have to follow that person's bowings. If you have a problem with that, practice and become the principal player next time. Learn all the solos just in case the principal player is suddenly unavailable.

In the absence of the principal player, the third chair player is expected to step up. The assistant principal usually sits third chair behind the principal. The inside players play bottom notes when in *divisi* (divided line), and the outside players are on the top notes. The inside players are responsible for page turns.

70 TUNING IN THE ENSEMBLE

In a symphonic orchestra, the ensemble customarily tunes to the oboe player's A, which is the same octave as your open-string A. String orchestras, and usually chamber groups, tune to the concertmaster (first violin section leader). Be aware that when an orchestra tunes onstage, this is merely a check. Players should have already tuned and warmed up thoroughly backstage.

If you play in an alternative ensemble like a rock band, check your open A with the keyboard. Also check your E with the guitar player's high E string. They should match, although an octave apart.

Wind ensembles and concert bands tune to B♭. Be aware that young wind players may need to be reminded to "push in" when sharp, and "pull out" when flat. Youth and amateur orchestras often tune the strings first to an A, followed by the winds tuning to a B♭. Percussionists can roll these notes on mallet instruments. If there is no oboe, the group can tune to the mallet percussion or a piano.

71 CLASSICAL GIG CHECKLIST

Be prepared. Check ahead and find out the expectations regarding proper attire. Most professional orchestras wear formal black, which means men in tuxedoes and conservative dressy for women. Chamber groups and amateur ensembles may wear black and white, or dark dress clothes. A black jacket is handy for both men and women, with pockets to store rosin, cloth, shoulder rest, etc. when entering and exiting the stage. If you play in an orchestra, always bring your music parts with your markings onstage and to rehearsal. Never assume that your stand partner will be there, much less responsible. If you missed a rehearsal, show up early to the next one and copy markings you may have missed. Check for new bowings, fingering suggestions, dynamics, cuts, or changes in repeats.

Bring business cards to your chamber ensemble gigs. Make sure your card includes contact information as well as the variety of events you cover, and instrumentation. Keep a music stand, a stand light, spare batteries, an extension cord, and black shoes in your car.

72 PLAYING AN OUTDOOR GIG

Sunglasses and insect repellent are necessary when playing out-of-doors. You should have a plan for rain and cold included in your event contract, indicating that you require shelter and temperatures at least 50 degrees Fahrenheit. If you have long hair, bring a hair tie/headband in case of extreme wind. Remember that black jacket from Tip 71? Keep it in your car on gig days in case you need an additional layer.

Music stands
While a folding stand may be lighter and easier to carry, a heavy concert stand won't blow over as easily during that wedding ceremony right by the lake. Three-page pieces are no longer an issue if you spring for stand extenders (about $10).

Clothespins
Bring extra clothespins for your friends. Remember that even an indoor gig may have a fan that blows your music around.

Plexiglass
Have a sheet of Plexiglass to put over your music to keep it in place. A sheet cut to 11" by 17" works well. This is much faster between pieces than moving multiple clothes pins, and provides extra weight to help keep the music flat.

Filler music
Be prepared for a wedding ceremony to start late. Other musicians may have car trouble, or a member of the wedding party could leave his tux pants in the hotel room. If you have fifteen minutes of extra music along, you can help the event go smoothly and end up with some solo gigs.

73 CONTRACT IDEAS

Regardless of the event, ask for half of your fee in advance, and the rest at the gig. List your client as "client," and yourself as "musicians' representative" on the contract. Don't list the other players' names, in case someone needs to get a sub. However, you may be asked to provide names for the program. Send your client two copies of the contract and include a self-addressed, stamped envelope. Instruct them to sign both copies, send you one, and keep the other for their records. Keep a default document for gigs handy, so all you have to do is plug in the dates and names. Have a rain clause ("shelter must be provided in case of rain"), temperature/snow clause ("musicians shall be provided heaters or will not perform in conditions below 50 degrees"), armless chair requirement (for a quartet or longer gig), and a cancellation scenario. Communicate with your client about repertoire. Let them know that there might be an additional fee if you have to purchase sheet music or do arranging for your group. If the wedding party requests a special song, they can buy the sheet music for you.

74 MUSIC BINDER

A folder for each instrument and style of music – classical, pops, and one with charts from a fake book – with the sheet music in the order of performance can help the event go smoothly. With the music in a three-ring binder, you can change the order easily for the next performance. Be aware that heavy binders do not work well with wimpy wire/folding stands.

75 JAZZ GIG CHECKLIST

Bring your ax (instrument) and amplification! If you are just jamming, the checklist is short. If your group has charts to read, you'll need a music stand, stand light, extension cord, and possibly a power strip. A fake book is good to have along for on-the-spot repertoire decisions and requests. Make sure you get a treble-clef version, such as *The Real Book*, Volumes 1–5, published by Hal Leonard Corporation.

76 ROCK GIG CHECKLIST

Have extra earplugs along, and one of your bandmates – or an audience member – will be forever grateful. Use headphones to warm up backstage, or plug into your tuner or electric violin. Don't forget your amp, patch cord, and spare batteries. A change of clothes, or at least a spare shirt, could be handy. Check Tip 77 for your extended list.

77 EXTRA! EXTRA!

Items for a variety of shows/concerts

Bring along an extra patch cord, a power strip, duct tape, set list, a folding chair, stand light, small flashlight, extension cord, amp, extra bow, spare set of strings, an old bridge, and a folding stand.

Always install new batteries into your violin, tuner, preamp, effects processor, flashlight, mic, etc. before the sound check. Have all your belongings labeled with your name or your band's name. When playing a show with multiple bands that may share drumsets, mics, amps, etc., items can end up with the wrong band. Even if your label is just marker or masking tape, it's better than losing something.

78 BUSINESS TIPS

If you want gigs, get started on your promotional kit and keep it updated. Include a binder or folder with plenty of business cards, rates, a demo CD (even if it is just excerpts), a list of available repertoire, and a performance calendar. Reviews and any other press clippings are helpful. Include a photo and members' bios on your website. Make sure all the pertinent information about your group is available through social media online, such as Facebook or Twitter.

Discuss with your regular ensemble members how often they would like to play gigs, and when they are available. Hire the most versatile players and have backup parts. If your violist is suddenly unavailable but your need to have a string quartet, have a violinist on third violin parts.

If you want to play mostly weddings, visit with florists, caterers, and wedding planners to propose a business arrangement. It could be as simple as posting each other's fliers or giving referrals. Couples who are engaged may put ads in newspapers or on college campus bulletin boards. Some college music departments have a list of available players for events.

79 SOUND CHECK

For electric/amplified gigs, be demanding. Tell the sound person how many channels you will need, and what your role is in the group. (Treat the violin like the lead guitar, voice, or backup/rhythm guitar.) Check the sound effects that you use most often. If your group has a drumset, understand that the drummer will need to check the amplification for each tom, the snare, bass (kick) drum, and cymbals, so bring a book along.

Once each instrument has been checked, the group needs to play together to get the balance levels set. At this point, it is beneficial to have someone out in the audience area to listen for balance, someone who knows how your group is supposed to sound. Don't hesitate to let the sound person know what you need to hear more and/or less of onstage.

No one wants to end up with tendonitis or surgery. If you are running late to a gig, there are stretches and exercises that you can do in the car. Your playing and endurance will improve if you warm up before playing and stretch after, especially in the winter. Stretch your legs, back, shoulders, neck, and hands.

Neck Stretch

Slowly move your chin toward your chest, and hold for a few seconds. Return your chin to normal. Next, move your left ear down to your shoulder. Do this often with the right ear, to counter the neck position required for holding the violin on your left side.

Shoulder Stretch

Raise both shoulders up as high as possible. Try to move them forward toward your jaw. Roll your shoulders down and back.

81 STRETCHES FOR ALL STRING PLAYERS

Stretch your legs before, during, or after a long rehearsal. Holding still in a chair for a couple hours is not ideal for your body. Get up and move around during the rehearsal break. If you want to practice something, play standing up. Your hamstrings, calves, and quads as well as lower back will probably need to move.

Car Stretch

I saw a guitar player do this one while driving! It impressed me, so I practiced it and now I can warm up in the car. Hold up your hand with all four fingers pointing up. Bend one finger down at a time, one joint at a time as possible

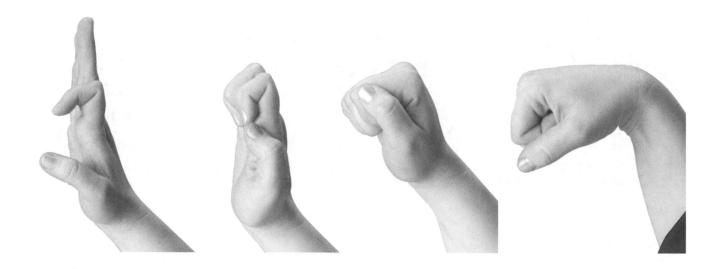

Hand Stretches

Make a tight fist for ten seconds, then relax and slowly point your fingers down. Next, extend all fingers out as far as pos sible and hold for ten seconds. Rest for a few seconds between exercises. You can also give each little joint of every finger a gentle massage.

Rest your hands flat on a table or countertop. Slowly raise the fingers of both hands up as high as possible. Relax after holding each up for several seconds. This exercise can be done with individual fingers as well.

Curl your fingers over so that the smallest joints are bent into a square shape. Curl the finger "boxes" down into fists, and then bend the fists over so your wrists are bent

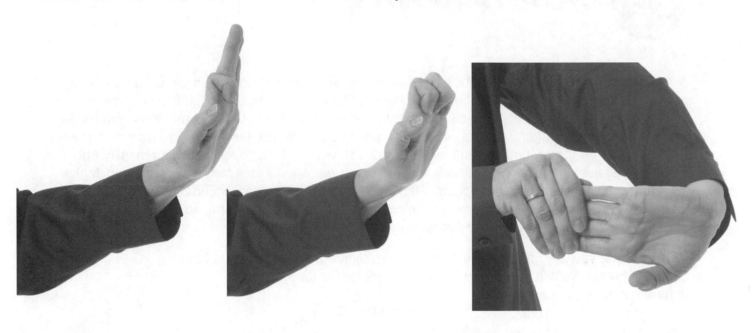

82 CHECK YOUR BRIDGE & BODY WHEN SEASONS CHANGE

When getting your car or home ready for winter, get your violin ready as well. Periodically check for warping, cracks, or opening seams as the temperatures and humidity levels go down. A seam is where two different panels meet. A crack on the front panel of your violin is much more urgent than an open seam. An open seam is a common occurrence, and quicker to repair. Some players use a winter bridge, which is installed around the first frost of the year. Any bridge adjustment or string changes can make the violin out of tune, so avoid having such work done close to a performance.

Bridge Adjusting Tip: Once you are a pro at replacing strings and adjusting your bridge, you might be ready to shave down the bridge a bit with light-grade sandpaper. Make sure you have a cloth between the tailpiece and the violin top. Next, carefully loosen the strings and remove the bridge. Just follow the original bridge shape, and don't sand down past the string notches. Rub the notches with graphite (pencil) before putting the bridge back on your violin. Plan ahead when reinstalling the strings. Examine the peg box to see which strings will pass below the others, and put those on first. You may want protective eyewear and gloves. Do your sanding over a garbage can.

83 HUMIDIFYING

A small sponge in a plastic container, such as an old prescription bottle, with small holes works as well as the commercial humidifier. The most popular brand is the Dampit. It is a sponge housed inside a rubber tube with holes to allow water to escape. You should use a humidifier if you live in an area that has a winter/dry season. The humidifier can keep your instrument from cracking when there is snow on the ground and the air is very dry. However, do not over do it. Your instrument can easily suffer water damage if the humidifier is too wet when it is inserted in your violin. Make sure that the sponge is wet, but squeeze it out so that no dripping can occur. Some humidifiers or instrument cases include a hygrometer, which measures the amount of humidity in the air. Other popular brands include Oasis and Planet Waves.

Winter Tip: If you are bringing your violin in from extreme hot or cold weather, allow it time to adjust. It should never sit in the car for too long, in direct sunlight, or next to a heating/cooling vent. Your violin may react to extreme changes in humidity as well as temperature, though this is usually less of a problem with newer instruments.

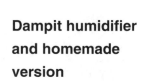
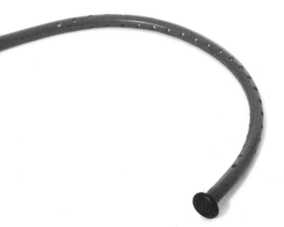

Dampit humidifier and homemade version

84 TAKE IT INTO THE SHOP

If something is rolling around inside your violin, your sound post has probably fallen over. The bass bar can also come loose. Take your violin to a repair shop as soon as possible. These are somewhat simple repairs, but one needs the proper tools and training. If you have open seams or a crack in your violin, be aware that whoever repairs it may remove the top panel. Your instrument could be in the shop for at least a few days.

Unexplained Rattle

There is nothing more frustrating than the unexplained rattle or buzzing sound! Check to see if part of a fine tuner is loose at the top or on the tailpiece. Look for the vibration in the pegs, purfling, seams, or the saddle or end button below the tailpiece. Make a note if the sound happens only in a certain range or on one particular string. Pickups can also make a buzzing sound. After you have exhausted all possibilities, take it into the shop.

85 PLAYING BY EAR

Even if your favorite song has no violin part, you can learn the melody, chords, or guitar solo. You may have to listen several times to get past the beginning, but have patience. Set small, attainable goals, such as being able to play along during the chorus section. Take notes about any changes that happen, using traditional notation, tablature, or whatever system you prefer. At least sketch out the number of verses, chorus, etc. Noticing the drums and bass will help you learn the song better, and will improve your ear.

If you have never played by ear before, start with something very simple, like "Mary Had a Little Lamb." Learn it in different keys, and experiment by flatting the third or fifth pitch of the scale used for the piece. Playing by ear will also help you improve your intonation.

A keyboard can be very useful if you want to figure out the chord progression of a song. Knowing the common form of most pop songs is also helpful: introduction, verse, chorus, bridge, etc. Each chorus and verse will usually have the same chords and melody.

86 PRACTICING ONE STEP AT A TIME

The most progress will happen with consistent practice. Fifteen minutes every day is better for retention than an hour once a week. To fix a mistake, you should be able to play it at least five times perfectly, or ten times if you really want it fixed. Recording yourself when practicing can be enlightening, if depressing. Play through a piece without stopping, as if it is a performance. Listen to the recording and circle all mistakes in pencil. Force yourself to fix the circled spots first, and then reward yourself by starting at the beginning. The next time you practice, start the piece in the middle or near the end, working on sections at a time. Always starting at the beginning results in knowing the beginning very well, but not necessarily the whole piece. An audience tends to remember the beginning and ending of a piece.

Keeping a practice record is a great idea, and it's not just for students. Immediately after a lesson is the best time to practice, because your teacher's suggestions are still fresh. Keep a violin journal. Take notes in it during or after a lesson. Also use it to keep track of what you want to accomplish and how much time you spend practicing.

87 RECORD & VIDEOTAPE YOURSELF

Nothing is more honest and unforgiving than a video or unedited recording of your own playing. The video can give you the benefit of seeing your posture, and what needs improvement. The audio recording is excellent, instant feedback about your tone, intonation, rhythm, and tempo. If you are working on intonation or rhythm, listen to a professional recording, watch a professional performance on the Internet, or – better yet – attend a professional performance and hear the piece live. You can also play a specific section on a keyboard, record it, then play it on your violin and compare the results.

88 PERFORMANCE JITTERS

The best way to defeat performance anxiety is to be well prepared and to perform at every opportunity. Get together often with friends and suggest a casual jam. Perform for parents, grandparents, friends, pets, et al. Young children can set up all their dolls or stuffed animals and do a mock concert. The idea is to visualize the performance scenario, just as professional athletes are mentally trained for performance. If you are afraid of playing alone, join a large amateur (non-auditioned) ensemble and start by sitting in the back on second or third violin parts.

A simple technique many performers use before going onstage is to breathe in and out slowly ten times. Be early to performances so you can take your time unpacking and warming up. Eat a light meal or snack near the performance area about an hour before playing, and keep a small bottle of water with you. Be aware of sugar, caffeine, and alcohol affecting your body before a performance. If you make a mistake, don't let it show on your face. Remember that the audience is there to enjoy an interesting performance, not to count your mistakes.

89 THE METRONOME IS YOUR FRIEND

A metronome can be your honest but annoying friend, who will help you keep a steady tempo. Start by practicing with the metronome at a slow tempo, and gradually speed it up. Make sure the metronome is loud enough, so that you can hear it and to stick with the tempo. Amplify it through speakers if necessary. Some well-known metronome brands include Korg, Intelli, Boss, Dr. Beat, Sabine, and Seiko.

A click track is often used in a recording studio. The click can sound like a cowbell, a hi-hat, snare drum, etc. Although usually beating the quarter note, the engineer can set it at the eighth note or elsewhere. Make sure the click sound is distinctive and loud enough. If your band is going to record with a click track, try practicing with one before recording.

Five things to keep in mind about your potential for a gorgeous violin tone:

- Bow distance from the bridge

- Bow speed

- Amount of bow used in the stroke

- Bow angle

- Pressure of the bow on the string

Most string players are told to use more bow to be louder. This is great advice, because many beginners, trying to avoid making a scratching sound, use too little bow. This scratching is often caused by a bow stroke that is too slow or that has too much pressure. Play with a fast but light bow on the E string; imagine the bow floating on the string. You can use a heavier bow stroke while playing on the D and G strings. Once you are comfortable with your sound, experiment with bow placement and speed.

Bow Angle/Straight Bow Tips: Place an empty paper towel tube on your left shoulder and use it to guide your bow. (This works well with multiple students.) You can also use a mirror. Check for a small triangle between your elbow, hand, and violin when you hold your bow at the frog. Pull the bow out halfway, and you should be able to see a rectangle. Once you are at the tip of the bow, you should see a long triangle. Another strategy is to make sure the bow remains the same distance from the bridge, no matter what part of the bow is being used.

Other factors that can change your sound:

- The bow hold, including pressure from the index finger

- The contact point on the string

- How much the bow has been tightened

91 SHREDDING

Shredding is a term often applied to guitar players who perform showy passages at blinding speeds. One way to achieve a similar showiness on the violin is to double, triple, and even quadruple your notes. For example, a melody made up of simple quarter notes can be made more exciting by playing each quarter note as two eighth notes, also called playing doubles, or as four 16th notes.

The following example shows "Twinkle, Twinkle, Little Star" in its traditional version, followed by a quadrupled version. You may notice that the basic melody and rhythm are the same, but the extra bow strokes on each note add a kind of showy variation.

TWINKLE, TWINKLE, LITTLE STAR
Traditional French Melody

TRACK 33

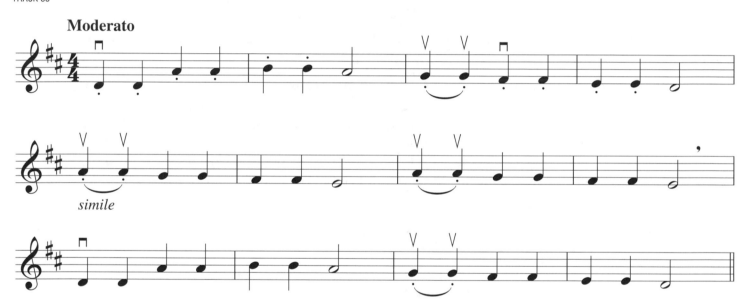

Moderato

If you have shredding chops, use them. String players can double eighth notes and make them into 16ths without the left hand working harder. Taking quarter or eighth notes and transforming them into 16th notes or a sustained tremolo can sound very impressive, especially to those who are unaware of a how a stringed instrument works. Even though a violinist may not need to stop and breathe, your audience might. Use your incredible technique sparingly.

92 PROTECT HEADPHONES A MUST!

Many violinists wear single-side headphones when recording: these cover only the right ear, and leave the left ear open for hearing the violin. Lacking the single-side headphones, players use regular headphones, but with the left side moved back so that they can hear their violin.

If you are playing in a live recording or without a click track (metronome), you may not need headphones. This is because the hollow body of some electric violins – and all acoustic violins – has vibrations of the back, front, and side panels as well as the bridge, strings, and sound post that allow us to hear the sound. Headphones are required, however, when playing an electric violin in a recording situation, especially if your instrument has a solid body. With a solid body electric violin, the pickup – usually in the bridge or is located under the bridge – is the only source of sound. The advantage of the electric violin is that one can practice unplugged while others are sleeping, or crank up the sound with a Marshall amp. The disadvantage is that if the electricity goes out, your solid body instrument will not be heard.

93 PROTECT YOUR HEARING

Hearing loss is permanent. Many violinists can experience hearing loss in their left ear, since the damage comes from length of time of exposure as well as intensity. Higher decibels cause more damage.

Foam earplugs are made of a compressed substance known as memory foam, which expands to fit once inside the ear canal. Silicone earplugs also conform to the ear canal's shape, and are popular with swimmers.

Be aware of volume when listening with headphones. If you can hear someone's music from several feet away through their headphones, their volume is too loud. Keep in mind that the volume at rock concerts often gets louder, especially once the headliner starts their set. The volume at the beginning of the show that didn't require ear plugs may end up at a very loud level.

94 TRANSCRIBING

If you want to improve your ear and notation skills, transcribe your favorite solo or song. Start with the basics. Listen to small sections at a time, and find out what pitches are being used. Large leaps between the notes or scale passages should be easy to hear. If you play a keyboard instrument, it may help with the notation. You can notate the rhythm and pitches separately, then put them together. Whether you use a computer notation program or scratch it out by hand, the process helps your musical development.

95 SINGING WHILE PLAYING

If you are determined to sing and play at the same time, make sure you can do both well separately. It seems obvious, but many players (pianists, drumset players, etc.) need to be reminded to practice certain things hands-separately before putting them together. Start with a simple rhythm or chord and strum on and off the beat. The easiest singing parts have a small range and are similar in rhythm to the instrumental part. Start by singing the same melody as you play on the violin. Be aware that your posture may change by opening your mouth wide enough to sing properly. Carla Kihlstedt (http://carlakihlstedt.com) is the master of singing while playing violin.

96 LISTENING

Listen to the great violinists, the best string players, singers, and guitar heroes. The more diverse your listening, the better your playing of different styles will be. Although listening to violinists is important, you can learn a lot from listening to great players on any instrument in any style, and apply something they do to your violin playing. Even classical musicians in most orchestras are expected to be able to play music from the Baroque, Classical, Romantic, Contemporary, and Post-Modern eras, and possibly Pops as well. Some of the best jazz players have a classical background and training, or vice-versa.

In addition to a listening library, many classical players have excerpt books for auditions. A great way to understand music you are learning is to buy the orchestral score, or borrow it from a music library. Listening to a recording while following along in the full score can help your reading and aural skills, so start looking in a university library or used-book store near campus.

97 VIOLIN STORAGE

Some players hang their violin or viola by its scroll on a music stand. Professionals never do this, because it is not safe. If you are in rehearsal and there is a break, it would be better to leave it flat on a chair than to hang it on a stand where it can easily be bumped. The best option is to keep your violin in its case, on the floor so it can't fall, when you aren't playing.

Anti-theft Tip: Never ever leave your instrument in the car, not even in the locked trunk. Never. Ever. Bring it in, wherever you go. Backpack cases are great for this.

98 VIOLIN TRAVEL

You can get permission for your violin case to be your carry-on, but call ahead to the airline and check the size of the plane. Have the measurements of your case handy, as some cases will not fit in the overhead. The current allowance of a carry-on plus a purse or laptop bag may also change.

The in-flight attendants may be more favorable and accommodating if you have only your violin and a very small laptop bag or purse that fits easily under the seat in front of you. Whether or not you plan to travel, have your instrument insured. Make sure you have the serial number, the estimated value, and your insurance information at home in case of the worst scenario.

99 VIOLIN RENTAL

It is practical to rent for the first year or so of your violin experience, especially for a child until he or she is ready for a full-sized instrument. Just like in Tip 16, find out what is included with the rental. Some stores have a rent-to-own policy, so that eventually you will have some collateral. Other places have a lease option, in which a portion of your rental fee goes toward purchase. Most rental instruments are for beginner or intermediate players. If you have rented for a couple of years, investigate buying a step up from what you are currently renting.

Pets and children can be dangerous for any instrument. A maintenance/breakage coverage plan is an excellent idea, even if your monthly payments are a bit higher. The plan may include new strings or repairs at a reduced price.

100 A BIT OF HISTORY

While the violin currently has the status as an icon of high art, it was once an instrument of lower standing among the string family. Traced back to 16th century Italy, the violin had a shorter, thicker neck, a flatter bridge, and a shorter fingerboard. Strings were gut prior to nylon, steel, etc. Its ancestors include the rebec, rebab (including the spiked fiddle), lyra, the viol, and the lira da braccio. These stringed instruments from different parts of the world had various sizes and shapes, as well as an assorted number of strings. While the Stradivari family is the best known of the master craftsmen, Amati, da Salo, Maggini, Stainer, Klotz, and Guarneri also contributed. Lutherie, the making of stringed instruments, has a strong tradition of apprenticeship.

The bow stick used to curve in the opposite direction (away from the hair) until François Tourte (1747–1835) revised it to today's standard shape. The newer shape, balance, and greater flexibility in the wood gave players much more power and technical ability. *Spiccato* and other bouncing styles developed as a result of the new bow design.

101 SURFING FOR VIOLINISTS

American String Teachers Association
www.astaweb.com

Darol Anger: fiddle
www.darolanger.com

Emilie Autumn: alternative, industrial, cabaret
www.emilieautumn.com

Cajun Fiddle
www.fiddlingaround.co.uk/cajun

Doug Cameron: jazz, rock, contemporary
dougcameron.com

Regina Carter: jazz, folk
www.reginacarter.com

Celtic Woman: all-female Irish ensemble; adult contemporary, new age
www.celticwoman.com

Papa John Creach: blues, rock
https://sites.google.com/site/pittsburghmusichistory/pittsburgh-music-story/blues/papa-john-creach

Charlie Daniels: fiddle, rock
www.charliedaniels.com

The Dixie Chicks: country, pop
www.dixiechicks.com

Double-stop Drone Recordings
http://fiddlersfolly.blogspot.com/2009/11/drones-and-double-stops.html

Electric Violins
www.electric-violins.net
electricfiddler.com

Fiddle Forum
www.fiddleforum.com

Folk, bluegrass resources including instruments and sheet music
www.folkmusician.com

Jerry Goodman: progressive rock, fusion
www.last.fm/music/Jerry+Goodman

Stéphane Grappelli
www.jazz.com/dozens/the-dozens-twelve-essential-stphane-grappelli-tracks

Richard Green: fiddle
www.richardgreene.net

Hampton String Quartet: rock sheet music
www.monalisasound.com

Christian Howes: jazz
christianhowes.com

Eddie Jobson: electric violin and keyboards; progressive rock and experimental music with Curved Air, Roxy Music, UK, etc.
www.eddiejobson.com

Nigel Kennedy: classical, jazz, klezmer
www.myspace.com/nigelkennedy

Carla Kihlstedt: classical, jazz, progressive rock, and experimental music
www.carlakihlstedt.com

Kenny Kosek: fiddle/bluegrass
kennykosek.com

Kronos Quartet: contemporary classical/experimental
kronosquartet.org

Brad Leftwich: fiddle
www.bradleftwich.net

Julie Lyonn Lieberman: improvisation, fiddle, jazz, blues
julielyonn.com

Vanessa Mae: classical, rock, pop
www.vanessamaeonline.com

Martha Mooke five-string viola; improvisation, classical, pop, rock
www.yamaha.com/artists/marthamooke

Mark O'Connor
markoconnor.com

NS Electric String Instruments
www.thinkns.com

Jean-Luc Ponty: fusion, jazz, pop
www.ponty.com

David Ragsdale violin and guitar; progressive rock with Kansas
www.davidragsdale.com

Rock Violin
www.fiddlingaround.co.uk/rock

Randy Sabien: jazz, bluegrass
www.randysabien.com

Robby Steinhardt: progressive rock with Kansas, Steinhardt-Moon
www.robbysteinhardt.com

Strings Magazine
www.allthingsstrings.com

Boyd Tinsley, Dave Matthews Band
davematthewsband.com

Turtle Island String Quartet: alternative/jazz
turtleislandquartet.com

Joe Venuti
www.redhotjazz.com/venuti

Violin blogs, interviews, etc.
www.violinist.com/

Vitamin String Quartet: rock and pop arrangements
www.vitaminstringquartet.com

Mark Wood: rock, heavy metal
www.markwoodmusic.com